Dedicated to these congregations who cooperated with their pastor in providing living laboratories in Christian wholeness and healing.

The Southern Hills United Methodist Church, Kettering, Ohio

The Columbia Heights United Methodist Church, Columbus, Ohio

The First United Methodist Church, Athens, Ohio

BLESSED TO BE
A BLESSING

Seabold United Methodist Church
6894 NE Seabold Church Road
Bainbridge Island, WA 98110

JAMES K. WAGNER

Blessed to Be a Blessing

THE UPPER ROOM
Nashville, Tennessee

Blessed to Be a Blessing
Copyright © 1980 by The Upper Room

Book design by Laura Wooten
Painting on front cover: *Grace* by Jerry Dunnam

First Printing, September, 1980 (7)
Second Printing, August, 1981 (5)
Third Printing, March, 1986 (3)
Library of Congress Catalog Card Number: 80-52615
ISBN 0-8358-0410-0

Printed in the United States of America

CONTENTS

FOREWORD

Perhaps I sounded as surprised as I was.

"How do you have healing services in the church, Jim?"

"Immediately following the morning service, all who wish to attend return to the sanctuary, and we have a service of healing."

I was intrigued, because at the time I did not know of another church where the healing ministry was so centrally placed in the corporate worship experience of a congregation. I was anxious to visit the church and experience this workable blend of public worship and public healing services in the church.

Almost six years ago I attended and participated in the healing service of Holy Communion, the anointing with oil, the laying-on-of-hands, and prayers for the sick. It was beautiful! The reason people attended was not for novelty or theatrics or to come into the presence of a superhealer with some special gift. They attended because the Body of Christ was alive, and as a part of the Body, they experienced healing and were instruments of healing ministry to others. They were there because the sacramental power of the gospel was alive. They were there because healing was occurring —

emotional healing,
physical healing,
interpersonal healing,
spiritual healing.

Healing is a vital part of Jesus' ministry. I asked Jim

to write this book because at The Upper Room we are committed to claiming (or reclaiming) the total sweep of the power of Jesus' ministry through the church in the world.

Dr. James Wagner has been conducting services of healing for ten years. He has now guided three successive United Methodist congregations in centering public services of healing in the ministry of the congregation. His graduate degree in the healing ministry of the church alongside his years of practical experience have led him to share this proven effective approach to Christian wholeness.

Danny E. Morris
Director, Developing Ministries
The Upper Room

PREFACE

He [Jesus] went about all Galilee, teaching . . . preaching . . . and healing.   Matthew 4:23

During the last half of the twentieth century, the healing ministry of the church has not only been aroused from generations of slumber, but now is calling for rightful attention along with the teaching, preaching, and discipling life of the Christian community. Many in the church today are taking a new look at this neglected arena of ministry. Consequently, we are discovering that healing was clearly taught and demonstrated by Jesus, practiced within the New Testament churches, and evident in the early centuries of Christendom's history.

In recent years, numerous books have been written on the subject of spiritual healing. In the annotated bibliography, I have included a number of helpful works dealing with the biblical and theological basis of healing, the relationship between medicine and religion, the wholistic understanding of health, and personal testimonies that vividly witness to God's healing love in action.

However, few of these volumes suggest practical and programmatic ways to have a healing ministry within the context of the local church. For this reason, I have written a "how-to" book for those Christians (lay and clergy) who are considering, who are ready to begin, or who are already having an intentional ministry of healing in their churches. The model I present for a healing ministry is one that I have developed over the past ten years and continue to use in my present pastoral ministry. This model I commend to you for the following considerations:

1. The model operates primarily out of obedience to Jesus Christ who is the same today as he was yesterday and will be forever.
2. It is dependent on the Holy Spirit, but not on any particular gift of the Holy Spirit (the exception being the gift of love, which is also classified in the New Testament as a "fruit of the Spirit").
3. It is sacramental in nature, incorporating confession, forgiveness, Holy Communion, anointing with oil, the laying-on-of-hands, and, at times, baptism.
4. The model is built on a team-ministry concept and does not depend on one person for "up-front" leadership.
5. It encourages interested and motivated lay persons to do more than "be ministered unto." It equips them to take leadership responsibilities.
6. It cooperates with God's desire for health and wholeness in body, mind, spirit, and relationships.
7. It does not claim to be the entire ministry of the church, but is comfortable and compatible with all the tasks of the local church (such as education, stewardship, social concerns, missions, evangelism, and worship).
8. The model benefits the entire congregation by encouraging those who are helped to serve the Lord of the church in other areas of ministry and need.
9. It is a common meeting ground for charismatics as well as non-charismatic Christians. Therefore, this is a unifying, rather than a divisive, ministry focusing on the healing, forgiving, empowering, reconciling love of Christ. Charisma without conflict within the Body of Christ is an attainable goal.
10. It is grounded in the local church, but open to the

entire community, fostering and welcoming ecumenical participation.

11. The model works closely with members of allied healing professions based on the belief that God uses many channels to help and heal persons (such as the medical profession, social workers, community helping agencies, and colleagues in psychology and psychiatry).

12. It could be incorporated into a wholistic health care center, in cooperation with the other healing professions.

A second reason for this book is the thirst in our times for experiential religion (personal encounter with divine reality). Large numbers of ex-church members and larger numbers of nonbelievers are searching for that "something more" outside the church. Ample evidence of widespread spiritual hunger is seen in the popular turning to Eastern religions, cults, and mind-altering drugs.

Yet the biblical narrative informs us that God is good, that God cares about his children, that communication with God is possible, and that experiencing God's healing presence is an everyday reality. Churches that offer opportunity for regular participation in a Christ-centered healing ministry are on target by coupling the needs of people with the God whose grace and resources are more than sufficient to meet those needs.

Because this is a "how-to" book, various kinds of help have been included. At the end of each chapter are discussion questions and suggested exercises designed for use by small groups who may be using this book as a study guide. In addition to a bibliography, I have compiled prayer suggestions, several liturgies for use in public healing services, and information regarding teaching tapes and conferences on spiritual healing. The list is by no means complete, but it points to practical help beyond this book for the Christian who is serious about the healing ministry of our Lord Jesus Christ.

I am truly indebted to a multitude of witnesses in the healing ministry of the church, and I have tried to be faithful in noting all materials quoted.

One of the serendipitous by-products of this writing has been the coming together of many Christians, most of whom had not met before, but all of whom were personally interested in the common quest for wholeness. Space and memory are too limited to name all the names. However, special appreciation goes to two ministers who demonstrated to me the validity of offering an intentional healing ministry within the context of a local church: the Reverend Robert Ward (First United Presbyterian Church, Middletown, Ohio) and the Reverend Donald Bartow (Westminster United Presbyterian Church, Canton, Ohio). Also, I thank Dr. Harold Platz, Professor of New Testament at United Theological Seminary, Dayton, Ohio, for stressing theological clarity. Now retired, Dr. Platz was my faculty advisor throughout the Doctor of Ministry program (1976-1978). Gratitude is extended to Danny and Rosalee Morris, "whobodies" whose love, prayer-support, and encouragement are a continuing source of refreshing joy.

Furthermore, I acknowledge my family, whose generosity made it possible for me to trade family time for typewriter time. Daily I thank God for three beautiful children, Laurie, Kerrie, and Toby, and for my supportive, reassuring wife, Mary Lou, who taught me through her personal example what it means to be blessed to be a blessing.

James K. Wagner
January 1, 1980
Athens, Ohio

INTRODUCTION

Have you personally experienced God's healing presence in your life? Have there been occasions of personal healings in body, in mind, in spirit, or in relationships when you knew without question the reality of Christ's love? If you can answer "yes," then give special consideration to one of God's covenantal promises to Abraham:

I will bless you . . . so that you will be a blessing (Gen. 12:2).

In the roller coaster history of Old Testament Israel, God's chosen ones often claimed Israel's privileges without following through with her obligations to be a blessing to the surrounding nations. Just as Abraham was instructed to share his blessings with others, likewise Jesus consistently encouraged persons he helped to help others.

As Christians, we sometimes fall into the narcissistic trap of thinking Jesus loves us more than he loves anyone else. Granted, his loving attentions to our personal problems do not hinge on how grateful we may be to him after the problem is resolved. He helps us, heals us, blesses us at the point of our need simply and magnificently because he loves us.

In the process of being healed or after health has been restored, the Bible clearly informs us that we are blessed to be a blessing. As Paul writes, "(God) comforts us in all our affliction, so that we may be able to comfort those who are in any affliction, with the comfort with which we ourselves are comforted by God" (2 Cor. 1:4).

As God called Abraham to walk the walk of faith, to leave behind the familiar, comfortable, secure routine, so through Christ is God calling you to walk the walk of faith, to leave behind the familiar, comfortable, secure routine. Experiencing his healing love and enabling power in your life comes not after all the difficult questions are answered; rather, only in risking for him by faith, trust, and obedience do you begin to know his salvation, healing, and wholeness.

Said the late Bishop F. Gerald Ensley (United Methodist) one day when he was being criticized for devoting so much of his attention to the cause of evangelism through the World Methodist Council and in every local church within his episcopal area, "My doing something is far better than your doing nothing."

So it is in the healing ministry of the church. The rewards are greater than the risks. The healings are more abundant than the failures.

Ask yourself these questions:

Would I like to be a blessing to someone?
Am I trying to be a blessing to anyone?
Who in my sphere of acquaintances are persons in need of Christ's healing?
Am I using my blessings and gifts and resources to help build up the corporate Body of Christ, the church?
Is the Lord of the church calling me, out of obedience to him, to be his cooperative instrument of health, wholeness, and salvation by beginning or continuing or supporting or participating in an intentional healing ministry?
Have I been blessed to be a blessing?

1

HE LEADETH ME

Jesus said, "I came that they may have life, and have it abundantly."   John 10:10

"I've been trying to ignore it, but healing through prayer keeps happening in my ministry." These words shared with me by a minister friend fresh out of seminary reminded me of my own questioning some twenty years ago. He went on to tell about a family in his church with a two-month-old baby. Doctors said the baby would die.

"I went to the hospital not knowing what to say or how to pray. Believing the child would be dead in a matter of days or weeks, I did not want to pray for healing, thinking failure to heal in that situation would cause the parents to reject God and to leave the church. So I made up a prayer on the way to the hospital — a general, nonspecific kind. But you know what? A funny thing happened! In the middle of my prayer in the hospital room with the parents and the baby, my mind went completely blank. All at once I found myself praying for the child's healing. Two weeks later, the family was in church having the baby, who had nearly recuperated, baptized. Now how do you explain that?"

Looking into his elated face I said, "I can't explain that except to say that my personal spiritual pilgrimage has taught me no longer to be surprised at the amazing good things resulting from prayer."

Because I, too, have experienced God's healing presence in the lives of persons whom I know personally, I decided in 1976 to enroll in a Doctor of Ministry program designed to study, to explore, to research, and to experience spiritual healing within the context of the local church. After completing my application, sending in my registration fee, and being accepted into the program, I became very ill five days before the intensive orientation week was to begin. Rarely do I get sick—one or two head colds a year, requiring no more than aspirin and rest. But this time it was different. It was the middle of August, and I realized I had the symptoms of pneumonia or worse. I loaded up with prescription antibiotics and went to bed, praying desperately that I would be well enough to get up, get dressed, and drive seventy-five miles by the end of the week.

However, as the time ran out, my condition got no better. I knew that if I missed this deadline I would have to wait another whole year before I could begin my graduate studies. But then an amazing thing happened. Mary Lou, my wife, in the middle of the night before I was to go out of town, knelt by my bedside, offered her own prayers on my behalf, and then we both went to sleep immediately. I awakened around 6:00 A.M., breathing normally, head cleared, and refreshed. I got up, showered, dressed, and was halfway packed when Mary Lou woke up.

"What are you doing?"

"I'm getting ready to go out of town for the orientation."

"That's ridiculous. You're too weak. You've been sick all week."

"I know, but the Lord must have used your prayers last night to strengthen me enough to go. So I'm going."

I cite this as another example of how the Holy Spirit can use our prayers in marvelous ways. But then, looking back over my life, I can now see the Lord's hand at work again and again. Baptized as an infant in the Roman Catholic Church, I spent the first six years of formal education in St. Boniface Parish, Piqua, Ohio. My father was Roman Catholic; my mother was a member of the Church of the United Brethren in Christ. I am very grateful for my early religious training and confirmation, received in the Roman Catholic Church, which faithfully and lovingly planted the gospel seeds. Through high school and college I remained active in the Catholic Church.

It was, however, my teenage association in the Young Men's Christian Association (YMCA) that first made an impression regarding the wholistic nature of the Christian religion. Through the YMCA program I came to appreciate the spiritual, physical, and mental dimensions of the faith.

After high school, I enrolled at Otterbein College, Westerville, Ohio, to earn a degree in Music Education. My goal at that time was to teach high school band and orchestra music. During my senior year at Otterbein, I decided to leave the Roman Catholic Church and experiment for one year being a Protestant. This decision was prompted by my falling in love with a beautiful coed who was active in the Evangelical United Brethren Church and whose father was an E.U.B. pastor. Neither of us wanted to have a religiously-mixed marriage, because we wanted a positive Christian influence in our marriage. She talked with my priest. I met with her minister for in-depth conversations. We both prayed, read, discussed, studied, and struggled. We also sought counseling with several ministers and professors whom we respected highly.

For several months we intentionally worshiped in "neutral" churches, such as Episcopalian, Lutheran, and Presbyterian. One of the influential books that helped clarify my thinking was Roland Bainton's *Here I Stand,* a biography of the sixteenth-century church reformer Martin Luther.

It was an exciting revelation to discover that Catholics and non-Catholics follow the same Christ, read the same

Bible, believe in prayer, faith, and responsible moral
living. Also, it came to me that the Lord of the church
never prescribed an organizational structure. He simply
but profoundly said, "Follow me." No institutional
church is perfect. No congregation or denomination has
a monopoly on spiritual truth.

My experimental year in Protestantism came to a
close with no regrets. Mary Lou Stine and I were mar-
ried five days after we graduated from Otterbein in June
1956, and I joined the Fairview E.U.B. Church in Day-
'ton, Ohio. Having minored in AFROTC, I had a three-
year active duty obligation in the United States Air
Force. Military orders called for me to begin my tour of
duty in December 1956. Thus I had five months of
uncommitted time following college graduation.

We were then living in Dayton, Ohio, only six blocks
from United Theological Seminary (E.U.B.). Because I
still had unanswered questions about the Christian religion, I made an appointment with the dean of the seminary and requested permission to enroll for the fall term
only. I told him I was not coming to the seminary as a
candidate for the ministry—rather as a seeker of spiritual truth. Request was granted. Thus I began my
intrepid entry into the theological community.

During our three years in the Air Force, we were
active in the air base chapels or in community churches
where we lived. We accepted the nomadic insecurities of
military life with positive attitudes. Looking back, I
believe God was actually preparing us for the United
Methodist itinerant ministry.

Toward the end of my Air Force obligation I began to
ask, "What's next?" We returned to Dayton, and I re-
enrolled in the seminary, because I felt a call to full-time
Christian ministry, a call I cannot define other than as a
gentle nudge by the Holy Spirit and warm encouragement by Christian friends and my supportive wife.

In June of 1962, I graduated from the seminary and
was ordained as an Itinerant Elder in the E.U.B.

Church. After serving two years as the associate pastor of the First E.U.B. Church in Westerville, Ohio, I was appointed to the Southern Hills E.U.B. Church, Kettering, Ohio, as the pastor of a congregation of more than four hundred members.

It was during this seven-year pastorate that I first became aware of the ministry of healing. I began to read newspaper and magazine accounts about main-line denominational congregations conducting healing services. Then in April, 1969, I learned that the First Presbyterian Church in Middletown, Ohio, was sponsoring a weekend healing mission with guest missioner Dr. Alfred Price, an Episcopal priest from Philadelphia. Because I was curious, I attended. I came home enthusiastic about this expression of ministry that I had been neglecting. It seemed this dimension is obviously present in Jesus' ministry as well as in his instructions to his disciples (the church).

I started reading everything I could find on spiritual healing, faith healing, and divine healing. My biblical studies revealed new insights into Jesus' healing ministry, and I found that the Greek word for *salvation* *(soteria)* could also be translated "health" or "wholeness."

I began to question seriously my style of ministry and the role of the pastor. It was during this time that I began to re-evaluate my professional ministry. Initially I had experienced satisfaction in my role as a "lone ranger," dedicated to helping people. For a while it felt good to be the "answer man" for my parishoners. But in time these roles grew wearisome. The Southern Hills Church had all the committees, commissions, and boards, as required by *The Book of Discipline of the United Methodist Church,* yet it seemed that as a pastor, I was carrying the weight of that church's ministry.

During the fall of 1968, I enrolled at Earlham School of Religion in Richmond, Indiana, to take a course in religious journalism, taught by Dr. Elton Trueblood, the

well-known Quaker author and Christian philosopher. I
learned much about writing, but, better still, I gained
insight into Dr. Trueblood's gifted understanding of the
church, of church renewal, and of the role of minister
and laity.

Dr. Trueblood is convinced that the local pastor is
primarily an enabler and multiplier of ministers (church
members). He believes the pastor's role is to encourage,
motivate, train, and enable Christians to do ministry—
not to do their ministry for them. He also helped me
recall that the church (the Christian movement) belongs
to the Lord of the church. Christ is the foundation, the
head, the cornerstone, the general manager, the executive director. The question is not, "What do I want the
church to be and to do?" The question is, "What does
Jesus Christ want his church to be and to do?"

All this tied in with my emerging awareness of the
larger dimensions of the gospel and the available spiritual resources for wholeness, salvation, and healing.

Another person who greatly influenced my rethinking
was Dr. Granger Westberg, a Lutheran minister who
has pioneered in the field of relating religion and medicine. Dr. Westberg's research into the problems of grief
revealed that at least 50 percent of the patients in hospitals have an unresolved grief experience that mani-
fests itself in physical and/or emotional illness. My family doctor also said he believed more than half the people
coming to his office have an emotional, mental, or spiritual problem that triggers their physical malfunctions.

As I began to put all this together, I experienced insight and personal healing. "Lord, now I know that the
church does not depend on me. Now I know that the
church depends on you and that I am completely dependent on you. What do you want me to do?"

As I studied churches and Christians who were active
in the healing ministry, I discovered two categories.
First, those Christians who have a gift of healing, many
of whom minister primarily outside main-line churches.

Second, those Christians who counsel and pray with
people for healing within established churches, not
necessarily claiming the gift of healing, but offering this
ministry of love and compassion out of obedience to
Christ.

I was definitely attracted to this second style of healing ministry. I began to share my understandings
through sermons and in small groups within the church.
With a handful of committed lay persons, we began, in
1970, to conduct monthly services of healing and Holy
Communion. From the beginning, I involved lay persons
in leading these services, in planning and evaluation ses-
sions, and in intercessory prayer groups.

In 1971, I was appointed pastor of the Columbia
Heights United Methodist Church in Columbus, Ohio,
with a membership near eight hundred. Because I had
experienced positive results in preaching, teaching, and
practicing the wholistic gospel, the healing ministry had
become an integral part of my theological understanding
of what it means to be a pastor and a Christian. Therefore, on the First Sunday in Advent, 1974, I started conducting weekly services of Holy Communion and healing, with strong emphasis on intercessory prayer
groups, lay leadership, and ecumenical participation.

When I was appointed to the First United Methodist
Church of Athens, Ohio, as senior pastor in June, 1978, I
naturally wanted to continue affirming the church's ministry of healing. With a receptive associate pastor,
David M. Griebner, and a willing congregation, we
started offering weekly services of Holy Communion and
healing on the First Sunday in Advent, 1978.

God gives each of us a personal history, uniquely different from the individual journeyings of other human
beings. I am convinced that God can use all our experiences (the good ones and the not-so-good ones) in uncanny ways when we give him permission to do so, and
when we go with the flow of his Holy Spirit from day to
day.

I do not consider myself to be gifted with special healing abilities; rather, I see myself more in the image of Henri Nouwen's "wounded healer,"[1] that is, one who recognizes personal limitations, wounds, and weaknesses, as well as strengths. Looking back, I am thoroughly amazed at how God has taken seemingly insignificant decisions, unimportant moments, unspectacular situations, and led me gently. I can only utter my own amen to the spiritual experience which Joseph H. Gilmore described:

He leadeth me: O blessed thought!
O words with heavenly comfort fraught!
Whate'er I do, where'er I be,
Still 'tis God's hand that leadeth me.

All those who say yes to Jesus of Nazareth — the timid and the bold alike — he calls into obedience to him. In our obedience, we become living conduits through whom he channels his health, his salvation, and his wholeness. Local churches have only begun to tap the spiritual resources for healing and for helping persons become whole by experiencing life abundantly.

GROUP STUDY GUIDE: CHAPTER 1

Materials needed for each participant:
    A sheet of plain white paper
    Pencils or pens
1. YOUR PERSONAL SPIRITUAL HISTORY
    The opening chapter deals primarily with the author's personal spiritual history. What about your personal spiritual history?
    Group Exercise
    a. Distribute paper and pencils to everyone. About halfway down the page of blank paper draw a line

---

1. Henri J. M. Nouwen, *The Wounded Healer* (Garden City, New York: Doubleday, 1972).

from left to right. At the far left of the line write
tho year you were born. At the far right pencil in
the current year.

b. Working individually (take three or four minutes), insert along your time-line three to six
events and dates that are significant in your
personal spiritual history.

c. Compare your personal data to the following
statement:
"God gives each of us a personal history,
uniquely different from the individual journeyings of other human beings. I am convinced that
God can use all our experiences (the good ones
and the not-so-good ones) in uncanny ways when
we give him permission to do so, and when we go
with the flow of his Holy Spirit from day to day.
. . . Looking back, I am thoroughly amazed at
how God has taken seemingly insignificant decisions, unimportant moments, unspectacular situations, and led me gently."

d. On the bottom of your time-line sheet, make a
note of any of the following that applies to your
spiritual journey: "insignificant decisions," "unimportant moments," "unspectacular situations."

e. Within the group share your insights about how
God has led you.

f. With the group, tell about the time when you
"gave God permission to do so."

2. INFLUENTIAL BOOKS
Roland Bainton's book on Martin Luther, *Here I
Stand,* helped clarify the author's thinking at a crit-
ical time in his spiritual pilgrimage.
Personal Exercise
On the back of your time-line sheet, write down
names of three books (other than the Bible) that have
influenced your thinking, attitudes, and behavior.
Group Exercise
Share with others in the group the names of the

books and tell briefly why these particular books were influential at the time.

3. INFLUENTIAL PERSONS

The author names several significant persons in his spiritual history.

Personal Exercise

Write down names of three persons (other than the immediate family) who have made a significant impact on your life.

Group Exercise

Select one of the names and tell how that person influenced you.

After all have shared, discuss the following question: Who is each of us influencing in a positive way? Be specific by naming someone and telling how.

4. THE CHURCH AND THE LORD OF THE CHURCH

Group Exercise

Discuss this statement:

"The church belongs to the Lord of the church. Christ is the foundation, the head, the cornerstone, the general manager, and executive director. The question is not, 'What do I want the church to be and to do?' rather, 'What does Jesus Christ want his church to be and to do?' "

Personal Exercise

Write your answer (on your time-line sheet) to the following: After our discussion, here is what I believe Jesus Christ wants the church to be and to do:

5. CLOSING PRAYER TIME

Form a circle and each person read his/her statement. Let the individual statements form a corporate basis for a time of prayer/commitment around the circle.

2
HEALING IS A BEAUTIFUL WORD

We know that in everything God works for good with those who love him, who are called according to his purpose.
Romans 8:28

When I enrolled in a Doctor of Ministry program with the goal of doing research and experimentation in spiritual healing within the context of a local church, my cautious faculty advisor asked, "Can you use a word other than *healing* in the title of your proposal? That is a loaded word and will raise red flags in the minds of many people." Upon learning of my project, a woman in our congregation said, "I think I like the idea, but spiritual healing scares people." An elementary schoolteacher (single, recent college graduate, active in the church) said, "I'll try to keep an open mind, but I warn you I'm skeptical."

Ridiculous as it may seem, a large part of the resistance to this significant area of Christian ministry is the pervasive, negative attitude toward the word *healing.* To speak of healing outside the context of the church is acceptable, but to suggest that the church should be involved actively in healing raises doubt and skepticism.

Why is there extensive, unavoidable skepticism among members of our churches toward spiritual healing? The answers to that question come easier than the solutions. Charlatan faith healers who have taken advantage of people come quickly to mind. Movie and television portrayals of ministers engaged in healing usually accent the dramatic, physical recovery while overlooking the other dimensions of health and wholeness. Even though Jesus and his early followers were active in the healing ministry, Christian education in recent generations has largely ignored the implications for today's church. Faith in modern medicine and the latest technology has replaced faith in God. Although pollsters continue to report that more than 90 percent of the American population believes in God, relatively few believe in a God who cares, loves, forgives, and heals. The task ahead is clearly defined — re-education on the significance, the importance, the necessity, and the practice of intentional healing ministry within the life of every Christian community (the church).

Let us begin with a biblical understanding of healing. Jesus understood and demonstrated the relationship between physical health, mental health, and spiritual health. The salvation Jesus offered included, but went beyond, spiritual well-being. Because he loved the whole person, his goal was to help each person become whole. Indeed, this wholistic view of persons and of God's redemptive action pervades and finds specific expression in the healing narratives. Clearly, the healings of Jesus were perceived as signs of God's ultimate redemption. This is expressed quite explicitly by Jesus:

If it is by the Spirit of God that I cast out demons, then the kingdom of God has come upon you (Matt. 12:28).

The English translations of the Greek New Testament text interchange freely "to heal," "to save," "to make well," "to make whole." For example see Matthew 9:21-22:

She said to herself, "If I only touch his garment, I shall be made well (whole)." Jesus turned, and seeing her he said, "Take heart, daughter; your faith has made you well (whole) (restored you to health)." And instantly the woman was made well (whole).

Wholeness (health) could be defined as the harmonious functioning of a person's body/mind/spirit. When one phase of this synergistic system breaks down, all parts are affected, and ill health results. The purpose of the healing ministry of the church is to help people maintain a healthy balance among body/mind/spirit (preventive medicine concept) and to assist in correcting an imbalance or to assist in making whole that which is broken or not functioning properly. Wholeness does not necessarily mean perfect physical health.

Becoming whole does not mean being perfect, but being completed. It does not necessarily mean happiness, but growth. It is often painful, but fortunately, it is never boring. It is not getting out of life what we think we want, but is the development and purification of the soul.[1]

Achieving health and wholeness is a lifelong process.

It is a process of finding, expressing, waiting, and rediscovering. God is wholeness, and the possibility of our becoming whole persons is a gift of God's grace.[2]

The greatest healing of all is the union or reunion of a human being with our heavenly Father (reconciliation with God). When this happens, physical healing sometimes occurs, mental and emotional balance is often restored. But without fail, spiritual health is enhanced and relationships are healed.

"The basic purpose of spiritual healing," according to Dr. George E. Parkinson, "is to deepen one's relationship with the living Christ."[3] Wholeness is not necessarily the same as "well-ness." A person can have a healthy relationship with God and neighbor and still not

1. John A. Sanford, *Healing and Wholeness* (New York: Paulist, 1977), p. 20.
2. Thomas A. Langford, *Christian Wholeness* (Nashville: The Upper Room, 1978), p. 9.
3. George E. Parkinson, *Spiritual Healing* (New York: Hawthorn, 1971), p. 2.

have perfect health in body and mind. A person may have a perfectly healthy body and mind and still be sick spiritually.

Although healing of the spirit is the primary goal in the spiritual healing ministry, we continue to seek wholeness also in body and mind and relationships. Our sin has been to assume that God is not interested in our mental, physical, and social health or to accept too quickly our various illnesses as fate, punishment, or bad luck. Each human being is basically a unity. Body, mind, and spirit are not independent entities which can be dealt with in isolation. What a person thinks influences physical health; the state of a person's spiritual health influences emotions and mental well-being. Feelings (positive and negative) influence body, mind, and spirit.

God, I believe, is a healing-loving-caring spiritual Creator who desires health, wholeness, and salvation for everyone. To support this faith-statement I look at my own experiences with this healing God. But, more, I consider what I know about the very nature of God and how God intended his sons and daughters to have abundant life.

The stories of beginnings in Genesis inform us not only that creation is "very good," but also that God provides humankind with everything necessary for a healthy, wholesome, happy life. The Bible, Old and New Testaments alike, consistently teaches God's goodwill toward all of his creation.

Other evidence of the Creator's desire for wholeness and healing is the natural tendency of the body to heal itself when sickness occurs. The medical profession cooperates with the anti-disease factors already present in each human being. Doctors are highly instrumental in assisting and promoting the healing process, but God does the healing. Yes, all healing comes from God, and all persons in the healing arts and sciences are conduits through whom God channels his goodwill. This is the reason the healing ministry of the church works closely with persons involved in medicine, surgery, psychiatry, psychology, and nutrition. For this reason the therapeutic value of religious faith and spiritual resources is truly appreciated by many members of the allied healing professions. Although spiritual healing does result in restored health, it is not a substitute for medicine or surgery or counseling. Cooperation—not competition—with the total needs of each person is the goal of the church's healing ministry.

God's valuing our well-being is also demonstrated through the person of Jesus Christ in healing the diseased person, in mending the broken and fractured relationships, in helping the helpless, in not throwing us away as so much worthless garbage, but rather in saving us. Jesus frequently emphasized God's goodwill toward us:

It is not the will of my Father who is in heaven that one . . . should perish (Matt. 18:14).

If you then, who are evil, know how to give good gifts to your children, how much more will your Father who is in heaven give good things to those who ask him! (Matt. 7:11)

However, God's will and God's desires are not always accomplished because he has given each of us a free will. When God decided to give us the will to do what we want to do, to act the way we want to act, to think the way we want to think, he placed some self-imposed, temporary restrictions on his power.

Does this mean that God is not omnipotent? No, God has the power to achieve his purposes, but he does not superimpose it on our will. God's omnipotence means that nothing can happen which can finally defeat him. The sin of disobedience in the Garden of Eden is illustrative of human will versus divine will.

If God did not permit us to function in life with free will and freedom in decision making, we would be little more than marionettes on his celestial string. Herein lie the agony and the ecstasy of belonging to the human race. Because God does not predetermine every step you and I take, we have unlimited possibilities for bad and good, sickness and health, death and life.

Dr. Leslie Weatherhead has the best explanation I have yet discovered of how God's will operates in the universe. Granted, it is presumptuous for anyone to say, "This is how God thinks." No human being can ever fully understand the mind of the Creator. You and I sense that we are probing a great mystery when we try to fathom God's will. It is mysterious, humanly incomprehensible, yet rational and trustworthy.

Dr. Weatherhead divided the nature of God's will into three categories:

1. The intentional will of God — God's ideal plan for humankind.
2. The circumstantial will of God — God's plan within certain circumstances.
3. The ultimate will of God — God's final realization of his purposes.[4]

In this matter of sickness and disease, the will of God — the original and intentional will of God for humankind — is good health in body, mind, and spirit. A healthy person is happier and more effective than a sick person. Therefore it is *better* to be healthy than to be sick. However, God's good intention for our good health may be thwarted. Some of the circumstances that trigger human sickness and brokenness are disease and accidents, mental and emotional disorders, sin and spiritual ill health. God does not intend for these kinds of circumstances to happen, yet when they do, defeat and failure do not necessarily follow.

As the apostle Paul so aptly put it, "We know that in everything God works for good with those who love him, who are called according to his purpose" (Rom. 8:28). It

---

4. Leslie Weatherhead, *The Will of God* (Nashville: Abingdon, 1977), p. 22.

is this faith-attitude that permits God's ultimate good will to be realized in and through and beyond life's unpredictable circumstances.

God's intentional will is for health, wholeness, and salvation; yet, when praying for healing, someone invariably quotes the words of Jesus in the Garden of Gethsemane, "Yet not what I will, but what thou wilt" (Mark 14:36).

The implication is that sickness can be God's will; therefore, some would say when praying for healing that we should always insert the "escape clause" from Gethsemane, "Not my will, God, but yours be done." Not so!

When Jesus prayed this prayer he was not seeking a personal healing; rather, he was a very healthy person trying to make a decision. Likewise, when we are looking for divine guidance in our decision making, then it is most appropriate to pray, "Not my will, God, but yours be done."

But in offering prayers for thanksgiving and forgiveness we do not use this phrase because we believe God's will is on the side of thanksgiving and forgiveness. Similarly, in matters of personal health and wholeness, we need not include the Gethsemane petition.

To develop an adequate understanding of healing within the church, we need to look closely at the wholistic style of ministry practiced by Jesus Christ. The Lord and head of the church always ministered to people at the point of their need.

The gospel narratives picture an itinerant Messiah who fed people bread baked in ovens as well as spiritual bread from his heavenly Father. Jesus was just as at home speaking to crowds as he was forgiving sins and curing various diseases and illnesses. Sometimes his healing method was a surgical word; other times it was a gentle touch.

When Jesus said, "I came that they may have life, and have it abundantly" (John 10:10), he was communicating his personal desire to enable people to become whole, complete, fulfilled persons and to live their lives as God intended life to be lived.

Why, we may ask, did Jesus minister in this manner? The answer is related to his understanding of the nature of humankind. Notice the message that has the highest priority with Jesus: "The time is fulfilled, and the kingdom of God is at hand; repent, and believe in the gospel" (Mark 1:15). Jesus clearly directs this call for conversion towards all humankind believing that all must intentionally turn their lives toward God because all have turned away from God. This is called sin. Is the situation hopeless? Not at all, because Jesus also firmly believed that humankind is the crowning jewel in God's creation. In response to this privileged position, humankind is obligated to produce lives that bear good fruit (Matt. 7:17-19). According to Jesus, men and women are created for service to God and to bring honor to God through their lives. Thus Jesus ordered his disciples to let others see their good works and glorify their Father in heaven (Matt. 5:16).

That large block of literature in the gospels that we call the healing ministry of Jesus records the signs of God's kingdom already breaking into the lives of men, women, and children. Jesus performed these concrete acts of love not to provide instant wonder cures, but mainly to demonstrate God's love, to present new possibilities for abundant living, and to encourage people to glorify God with a new heart, a new commitment, and a new loyalty.

Jesus operated on the assumption (as does medical research) that disease is not beneficial to the human race. Jesus believed all disease is evil in origin and opposed to the kingdom of God. Disease is not to be accepted; it is to be fought and conquered. Notice Jesus never blames his heavenly Father for a person's illness, nor does he suggest that sickness is God's way of disciplining wayward persons. Jesus never told anyone,

"Your sickness is God's will," or, "God made you sick to test your faith."

Francis MacNutt, a Roman Catholic, points out:

Never do we find that Jesus, in the presence of sickness, encourages people to accept their sickness, nor does Jesus give them sermonettes on patience and endurance. But instead, His example was that every time He met sickness, He treated it as evil.[5]

Jesus made it quite clear that his followers are to engage in these same healing ministries. In his commissioning of the seventy, his instructions are: "Heal the sick . . . and say to them, 'The kingdom of God has come near to you' " (Luke 10:9). In his parting messages, he is even more explicit:

Truly, truly, I say to you, he who believes in me will also do the works that I do; and greater works than these will he do, because I go to the Father (John 14:12).

The scriptural authority for the church to engage in healing ministry is not lacking. What is noticeably absent is obedience to the Lord of the church in offering ourselves to be faithful channels for his healing love. Few can claim the gift of healing, but all Christians have been given the privilege of obeying his commands and trusting to him the outcome. To a large gathering of United Methodists in Louisville, Kentucky, Francis MacNutt said, "Every Christian can heal. You don't have to have any special gift. Just love Jesus, pray for persons, and healing happens. That way seems to work as well as the fantastic gifts of famous faith healers."[6]

The word of God is calling, demanding our attention and action in the healing ministry of the church today:

---

5. Francis MacNutt, quoted in Sept. 1976 issue of a monthly publication by the Westminster Presbyterian Church, 171 Aultman Avenue N.W., Canton, Ohio 44708.
6. Francis MacNutt, quoted in *The United Methodist Reporter*, August 17, 1979, page 1.

Jesus Christ is the same yesterday and today and forever (Heb. 13:8).

Cast all your anxieties on him, for he cares about you (1 Pet. 5:7).

Is any one among you suffering? Let him pray.
Is any cheerful? Let him sing praise.
Is any among you sick? Let him call for the elders of the church, and let them pray over him, anointing him with oil in the name of the Lord;
And the prayer of faith will save the sick man, and the Lord will raise him up;
And if he has committed sins, he will be forgiven.
Therefore confess your sins to one another, and pray for one another, that you may be healed.
The prayer of a righteous man has great power in its effects (James 5:13-16).

Yes, *healing* is a beautiful word and a beautiful experience, both inside and outside the church community. Our task, if we are to be faithful to Jesus Christ, is to affirm and to cooperate with the intentional will of God for wholeness and a harmonious functioning of the body/mind/spirit relationship.

God's desire for our good health is already manifested in hospitals, in doctors' offices, in various schools of counseling therapy, in private homes where small groups of Christians gather for prayer, and in spiritual healing conferences held in public buildings, convention centers, and football fields.

Why not bring healing back into the church?
Why not allow the healing Christ to touch and help his people in his church?
Why not have public healing services in the sanctuary of the church?

GROUP STUDY GUIDE: CHAPTER 2

Materials needed for this session:
    Chalkboard and chalk
    The text

"Why not have public healing services in the sanctuary of the church?" There are some negative attitudes
that keep this from happening and some positive factors
that support this happening. Let's look at both.

1. NEGATIVE ATTITUDES TOWARD HEALING IN
   THE CHURCH
   Four negative factors are named:
   a. Charlatan faith-healers
   b. Accenting only the dramatic, physical healings
   c. Faith in medicine has replaced faith in God.
   d. Lack of education in the church on spiritual heal-
      ing
   Group Exercise
   As a group, list on the chalkboard five or six additional reasons why Christians resist spiritual healing
   and the process of conducting public healing services
   in the church.
   Next, select from the group's list the three most
   significant factors and put a 1, 2, or 3 by the first,
   second, and third choices of the group.

2. BASIC PURPOSE OF SPIRITUAL HEALING
   Before coming to the positive factors, first look at
   an intriguing thesis on healing. According to Dr.
   George E. Parkinson, "The basic purpose of spiritual
   healing is to deepen one's relationship with the living
   Christ."
   Group Exercise
   Within the group, discuss whether you agree or dis-
   agree with this statement.
   As a group, list five additional purposes of healing
   (apart from "getting well") and write them on the
   chalkboard.

3. POSITIVE FACTORS FOR HEALING IN THE
   CHURCH
   a. *Wholeness and well-ness*
      The church advocates both wholeness and well-
      ness. Wholeness is not necessarily the same as
      well-ness. A person can have a healthy relation-

ship with God and neighbor and still not have perfect health in body and mind. A person may also have a healthy body and mind and still be sick spiritually. The church is for both.

Group Exercise

Using the author's definition of *wholeness* on page 29 discuss the relationship (or the lack of it) between spiritual wholeness and physical wellness.

b. *The will of God*

The church seeks understanding of the will of God. Dr. Leslie Weatherhead describes God's will in three categories:

1. God's intentional will
2. God's circumstantial will
3. God's ultimate will

Personal Exercise

Take a couple of moments for reflection about which of these three categories has most directly impacted you.

After reflection, each of you may wish to share your thoughts.

c. *Abundant life in Christ*

Jesus said, "I came that they may have life, and have it abundantly" (John 10:10). He was communicating his personal power which enables people to become whole, complete, fulfilled persons and to live their lives as God intended life to be lived.

Personal Exercise

Share one personal "abundant life/healing" experience.

d. *Every Christian can heal.*

The church has not always emphasized the healing ministry of every Christian. But many strong voices in the church are helping bring a strong healing emphasis.

Personal Exercise

Select one of the two following statements to respond to:

1. The reason I have not been involved in healing ministry is . . . .
2. The reason I have been involved in healing ministry is . . . .

4. ACCENT THE POSITIVE

There are enough negative attitudes in the church to restrict healing ministry. But there are many positive factors which cause the church and the Christian to be involved in healing.

a. The church advocates both wholeness and wellness.

b. The church seeks understanding of the will of God.

c. Jesus brought us "abundant life."

d. Every Christian is called to heal.

Group Exercise

List on the chalkboard:

a. Three reasons *why we should* bring healing back into the church.

b. Three reasons *why we should* allow the healing Christ to touch and help his people in his church.

c. Three reasons *why we should* have public healing services in our church.

5. CLOSING PRAYER TIME

As a group, incorporate the data gathered in previous group exercises in a closing prayer time for healing in the church.

3
THE SACRAMENTAL MODEL

The cup of blessing which we bless,
is it not a participation in the blood of Christ?
The bread which we break,
is it not a participation in the body of Christ?

1 Corinthians 10:16

Consider the sacramental model for public healing services in the church. By this I mean directing the central focus of the worship experience on the Lord Jesus Christ who has already given to us visible signs of his invisible grace. He has already commanded his church to do certain things in memory of him, not in the mood of a fallen hero's funeral, but rather in the joyous spirit of celebrating victorious good news. Because the heartbeat of the healing ministry is the living Christ, whose loving presence is the same today as it was yesterday and will be tomorrow, let us intentionally focus upon him.

Sacraments ordained of Christ are not only badges or tokens of Christian . . . profession, but rather they are certain signs of grace, and God's good will toward us, by which he doth work invisibly in us, and doth not only quicken, but also strengthen and confirm, our faith in him.[1]

The Sacrament of Holy Comment of Holy Communion

For many Christians, the sacrament that consistently brings them directly into personal contact with Jesus Christ is the sacrament of Holy Communion. The Lord's Supper, or the Eucharist, as understood and practiced

---

1. United Methodist *Book of Discipline*, Article XVI (Nashville: The United Methodist Publishing House, 1976), p. 59.

among Christians today, is one of Christ's healing gifts to his church. I have discovered positive receptivity and quicker acceptance of the spiritual healing ministry within the congregation when the sacrament of Holy Communion is incorporated into the public healing service.

Why is this? What inherent factors contribute to healing during the congregation's participation in Holy Communion?

St. Paul points us toward some of the answers:

I received from the Lord what I also delivered to you, that the Lord Jesus on the night when he was betrayed took bread, and when he had given thanks, he broke it, and said, "This is my body which is for you. Do this in remembrance of me." In the same way also the cup, after supper, saying, "This cup is the new covenant in my blood. Do this, as often as you drink it, in remembrance of me." For as often as you eat this bread and drink the cup, you proclaim the Lord's death until he comes. (1 Cor. 11:23-26)

The cup of blessing which we bless, is it not a participation in the blood of Christ? The bread which we break, is it not a participation in the body of Christ? (1 Cor. 10:16)

Even though this participation, this remembrance, this covenantal relationship defies satisfactory verbal explanation, the faithful Christian does experience direct contact with the Source of life, health, salvation, and wholeness.

Paul purposely ties together the Lord's Supper with the death, resurrection, and coming again of Christ. For Paul, worshipful moments of Holy Communion are dramatic reminders of the total gospel message rooted in the atonement made possible by Christ's death on the cross.

While all explanations of Christ's atonement fall short, the Christian's acceptance and appropriation of that atonement occur every day. To be "at one" with God in Christ is to be healed at the deepest and most significant levels. In our daily journey toward wholeness in body, in mind, in spirit, and in all relationships, we need sacramental grace again and again.

Sacramental grace is personal grace. Although produced by means of physical instruments, it is not contained in them. It is not produced by these instruments, but by means of them, and it is Christ who produces it by making use of them, just as He makes use of the human word to encounter men and reach them at the level of their humanity.[2]

We cannot overstate the health-producing effects of the sacrament of Holy Communion. To participate in faith in the breaking of the bread and the drinking of the cup is to participate in the incarnation, atonement, redemption, and resurrection of Jesus Christ. To become "at one" with him always promotes health and wholeness.

Other positive factors related to Holy Communion are the traditional prayers, the familiar scriptures, and the eating and drinking in faith with thanksgiving. Communion liturgies of all Christian denominations incorporate confession, forgiveness, words of assurance, and pardon. Because our attitude and receptivity are so crucial in the healing process, "The Prayer of Humble Access" offered in unison by the congregation is especially therapeutic:

We do not presume to come to this thy table, O merciful Lord, trusting in our own righteousness, but in thy manifold and great mercies. We are not worthy so much as to gather up the crumbs under thy table. But thou art the same Lord, whose property is always to have mercy. Grant us therefore, gracious Lord, so to partake of this Sacrament of thy Son Jesus Christ, that we may walk in newness of life, may grow into his likeness and may evermore dwell in him, and he in us. Amen.[3]

This built-in objectivity of the sacrament of Holy Communion helps the participant focus on Christ rather

---

2. Oscar Cullmann and F. J. Feenhardt, *Essays on the Lord's Supper* (Atlanta: John Knox Press, 1975), p. 80.
3. *The Book of Worship* (Nashville: The Methodist Publishing House, 1964), p. 20.

than on the presiding clergy. The object of our faith is Christ, not the worship leader. The invitation is to come to Christ, not to the liturgist.

Such matters as open or closed communion, who is authorized to administer the sacrament, and at what point in the liturgy the sacrament is to be celebrated will be determined by denominational tradition and doctrine. Some ministers prefer to have individual prayers for healing followed by a celebration of the Holy Communion, as an act of thanksgiving and affirmation of faith in the healing Christ.

I prefer to invite the congregation to come forward to kneel or to stand around the communion table and to receive the bread and the cup in a manner accustomed to them. Then, the communicants are given the option of returning to their pews after receiving the elements or remaining at the communion railing in a worshipful attitude for the anointing with oil and the laying-on-of-hands with prayer for personal needs.

Anointing with Oil

We can pray with people for healing without anointing them with oil. In fact, many churches do conduct public healing services without using oil. What, then, is the intent and purpose of incorporating this physical element into the spiritual healing ministry?

In biblical times, oil (usually olive oil) was universally considered a medicine. References to anointing occur throughout the Bible: 143 in the Old Testament and 20 in the New Testament. Some of these passages deal with consecrating leaders and kings.

Our concern here is with the anointing of the sick with oil for healing, which was a common practice in Jesus' day. In the parable of the Good Samaritan, the injured man was treated by having oil poured on his wounds (Luke 10:34). The twelve apostles used oil: "They . . . anointed with oil many that were sick and healed them"

(Mark 6:13). The instruction of James to use oil when praying for the sick was simply an order to employ the best medicine available along with prayer (James 5:14). This passage implies that prayer and medicine go together. A reasonable implication is that when the doctor gives us a prescription we should take the medicine accompanied with prayer. I know a registered nurse who intentionally prays over the pill cart she wheels in and out of the hospital rooms invoking the Lord's blessing on the patients through the medicine.

The oil used in public healing services has no mystery or magic about it. The oil has no healing characteristics of its own. Rather, anointing the forehead in the sign of the cross is a sacramental symbol invoking the healing love of the triune God: Father, Son, and Holy Spirit. The symbol points beyond itself to the presence of the healing Christ in a moment of holy communication.

For me not to use oil in public healing services would be as unnatural as not using bread and wine in Holy Communion. These physical symbols are powerful, dramatic, therapeutic communicators of God's love and healing power at work in our lives.

One woman said, "After coming to the healing service and being anointed, I do not wash my forehead for two or three days. By touching and feeling the oil, I am reminded of Christ's healing in my life."

Jesus' disciples had no hesitancy in using oil, nor did the New Testament churches. The regular use of oil as a sacramental symbol of God's operative grace is valid and appropriate today.

The Laying-on-of-Hands

Another significant practice in the church's healing ministry is called the laying-on-of-hands with prayer. Lest we shy away from this biblical practice, recall some of the ways we communicate through physical touch today. The instinct is strong to reach out and touch those whom we wish to greet or to sympathize with, or those we wish to comfort. Our hands do communicate a healing touch: the restless child becomes quiet; the distraught person is made aware that someone cares; the handshake shows acceptance rather than rejection.

Our natural desire to communicate caring for others through our hands is further enhanced by the example and frequent practice of Jesus. The touch of Jesus' hand made such a significant difference in so many people's lives that the authors of the gospels mention this repeatedly (see Matt. 8:1-4, 14-15; 9:18-26; 19:13-15; Mark 1:28-31; 40-45; 5:21-43; 6:1-6; 7:32-37; 8:22-25; 9:14-29; 10:13-16; Luke 4:38-44; 5:12-16; 8:49-56; 13:11-17).

Early Christians employed the laying-on-of-hands in the ordination of deacons, in the commissioning of missionaries, in receiving the baptism of the Holy Spirit, and in healing (see Acts 3:7; 6:6; 8:17; 9:17; 19:6). The laying-on-of-hands was regarded as one of Jesus' fundamental teachings: "Therefore let us leave the elementary doctrines of Christ and go on to maturity, not laying again a foundation of repentance from dead works of God, with instruction about ablutions, the laying on of hands, the resurrection of the dead, and eternal judgment. And this we will do if God permits" (Heb. 6:1-3). Because of the obvious biblical precedent coupled with our natural desire to reach out to people in need, we should not hesitate to touch gently and lovingly those who ask for healing prayers. The focal point continues to be on the healing Christ, with clergy and laity alike offering their hands, their faith, their love, and their compassion to be the channels for the divine Physician to do his work among us.

Recently I asked several people who came forward for anointing and the laying-on-of-hands if they remembered the prayers offered on their behalf. One person responded, "No, I cannot recall the words, but I remembered all week the warmth, the love, the atmosphere of care as people gathered around me and prayed for my healing."

The laying-on-of-hands is a tangible expression of Christ operating in and through us as we minister in his name. It is another avenue for his sacramental grace.

Take a moment now to meditate on this prayer for healing:

These hands are laid upon you in the Name of the Father, the Son, and the Holy Spirit. May the power of His indwelling presence heal you of all infirmities of mind, body, and spirit, that you may serve Him with a loving heart. Amen.[4]

GROUP STUDY GUIDE: CHAPTER 3

Materials List:
    Small bottle of olive oil
    Bibles for each participant
1. THE SACRAMENT OF HOLY COMMUNION
    For many Christians the sacrament that consistently brings them directly into personal contact with Jesus Christ is the sacrament of Holy Communion.
    Personal Exercise
    Share (one or more persons in the group) about a healing of the body or the mind or the spirit or in relationships that occurred while participating in this sacrament.
    Group Exercise
    Turn to the "Prayer of Humble Access" on p. 42, and read it aloud as a group. Discuss what is therapeutic in this healing process/prayer.
2. ANOINTING WITH OIL
    The regular use of oil as a sacramental symbol of God's grace is valid and appropriate today.

---

4. Don Bartow, *The Spiritual Healing Ministry,* Article 3, July 1970, Westminster United Presbyterian Church, 171 Aultman Avenue N.W., Canton, Ohio 44708.

Group Exercise

Select one person in the group to invite participants who wish to, to be anointed with oil with this prayer, making the sign of the Cross on the forehead:

"May the spirit of Jesus live in you and make you whole in your body, your mind, your soul, and your relationships."

Amen.

3. LAYING-ON-OF-HANDS

This is a central expression of the church's healing ministry.

Group Exercise

a. *Human touch can convey a message of caring.*

Our hands do communicate a healing touch; the restless child becomes quiet; the distraught person is made aware that someone cares; the handshake shows acceptance.

Stand in a tight circle facing the center.

Everyone turn a 90-degree angle to the right.

Place your hands on the person's shoulders in front of you.

Take a few moments to gently massage the neck, shoulder, and back. Then about-face 180° and repeat the process.

After a few moments, sit down and discuss:

1. How are you feeling right now?
2. What was being communicated through our hands?

b. *Bible study and discussion about Jesus' touch.*

After distributing Bibles to participants, select one or two of the following passages to be read aloud to the rest of the group: Matthew 8:1-4, 14-15; 9:18-26; 19:13-15; Mark 1:28-31, 40-45; 5:21-43; 6:1-6; 7:32-37; 8:22-25; 9:14-29; 10:13-16; Luke 4:38-44; 5:12-16; 8:49-56; 13:11-17.

Discussion: What do these biblical texts inform us about Jesus' practice of using hands in the healing process?

c. *Laying-on-of-hands with prayer.*
There is a dimension of the practice of laying-on-of-hands that we cannot know by talking or reading about it. To fully appropriate the dynamic, you must experience it. Here is a beginning approach to this practice. (Note: If any of you in the group does not feel comfortable with the following procedure, you may observe.)

1. Inquire if anyone has a personal need for healing of body, mind, spirit, or relationships which they would like prayer for.
2. Invite that person to sit on a chair placed in the middle of the group.
3. All who wish to participate gather around and while gently touching the person with loving compassion on the shoulder or head or hand, have one of the group members pray this prayer: "These hands are laid upon you in the name of the Father, the Son, and the Holy Spirit. May the power of his indwelling presence heal you of all infirmities of mind, body, and spirit, that you may serve him with a loving heart. Amen." (Pause in silence.) (Others may want to offer brief, spontaneous prayers for healing as prompted by the Holy Spirit.)
4. If more than one requests this ministry, praise the Lord and repeat the laying-on-of-hands prayer experience.
5. Take time to discuss this prayer experience.

4. CLOSING PRAYER TIME
Conclude this session by standing in a circle, holding hands, and praying together the Lord's Prayer.

4

THE PUBLIC
HEALING SERVICE

Is any among you sick? Let him call for the elders of the
church, and let them pray over him, anointing him with oil in
the name of the Lord.   James 5:14

All Christian worship is beneficial and helpful. Why
have a special service of healing? This frequently-raised
question overlooks the reality of what happens—and
what does not happen—in an average Sunday morning
service. Although it is true that whenever two or three
or more gather in the name of Jesus Christ many good
things happen, the typical Sunday morning liturgy does
not focus intentionally or specifically on God's desire and
power to heal. Ideally every occasion of Christian corporate worship should offer opportunity for healing
prayers. The ideal is far from reality in the majority of
today's congregations. We have special emphases on
evangelism, stewardship, baptism, confirmation, The
Lord's Supper, Christian education, missions, social concerns, and other areas of the gospel. Why not have special times and services in the church to center on the
spiritual resources for healing?

A regular, public healing service is a powerfully effective witness to the entire congregation and the larger
community that God is the source of all healing. Some
ministers and lay leaders hesitate to begin public healing
services because they feel they do not possess the gift of
healing. Donald Bartow, a United Presbyterian pastor in

49

Canton, Ohio, has had an active spiritual healing ministry since 1959 and firmly believes:

> The charismatic gift of healing is not a requirement for the Ministry of Healing, but faithfulness on the part of each Christian is the indispensable factor. No special gift of healing is needed for one to begin the Spiritual Healing Ministry because our aim is to lead all to the Great Physician, Jesus Christ. It is not our ability but our availability that is desired. Jesus Christ will do the work and supply the power.[1]

The key word, then, is *obedience.* As Bartow puts it, when it comes to healing ministry in the church, "an ounce of obedience is worth a ton of Bible study."[2]

In his commission of the seventy, Jesus instructs them to "heal the sick . . . and say to them, 'The kingdom of God has come near to you' " (Luke 10:9). Jesus called all Christians (lay and clergy alike) to obey and to be available in his healing ministries.

How to Get Started

The following guidelines are based on my personal experiences in starting intentional healing ministries in three different churches.

Prior to announcing the first public healing service, the minister needs to have carefully informed the congregation about his or her interest in the healing ministry. This may come through a series of sermons based on any of several biblical healing events, a series of personal articles written in the church newsletter, and informal conversations with adult groups in the church. Crucial in the preparation stage is the discovery of church members who are interested in and receptive to learning more about spiritual healing. This could be

---

1. Don Bartow, *The Healing Service* (Canton, Ohio: Life Enrichment Publishers, 1974), p. 15.
2. From a lecture on Spiritual Healing by Don Bartow at the Westminster United Presbyterian Church, Canton, Ohio, Oct. 18, 1977.

accomplished by offering a short-term study group on the subject, bulletin inserts with response guides soliciting written comments to the sermons on healing, or simply a direct invitation to interested persons to contact the pastor for exploratory conversations. A spiritual healing ministry that is primarily initiated, organized, sustained, and solely led by the minister will have limited influence in the life of the congregation. Lay leadership must be involved in the preparation and in every facet of the healing ministry. Training and leadership opportunities need to be offered to motivated, concerned lay persons.

When word gets around that plans are being formulated to hold public healing services in the church, the response will range broadly from surprise to misunderstanding to apathy to acceptance. I have found it best, when initiating a healing ministry in a local church, to announce quite early in the preparation stage that this will be an experimental form of ministry. This means setting a time limit and establishing ways to evaluate the experiment. Congregational governing bodies and official boards are more apt to cooperate on this basis.

I suggest an initial time-frame of two to three months with the assurance given that evaluations will be made. Toward the end of the time-frame, return to the governing body of the church with reportable data and recommendations. In my present pastorate, this has been a successful approach. The associate minister and I recommended to the Administrative Board that we be given permission to conduct weekly services of Holy Communion and healing beginning the first Sunday of Advent and continuing through the Epiphany season. Permission was granted with the provision that we report back to the Board toward the end of the experimental time period. Based on the positive responses received in writing from the participants, we then recommended that our church continue to offer weekly services of Holy Communion and healing with the option to experiment with different times and days of the week. Permission granted. Today the healing ministry is officially accepted and well integrated into the total program of our church.

Doing the Experiment

After the decision is made to begin, other questions arise for consideration and action:

What type of worship service should it be? Formal or informal? Liturgical or non-liturgical? With or without anointing oil?

How frequently should the services be held? Who will lead the services? What time of the week? Which room in the church? What if nobody comes? What do we do with the people who do come?

My survey of churches currently engaged in public healing services reveals a vast assortment of styles, liturgies, and methods. Much can be gained by visiting, observing, and participating in healing services held in different churches. In addition to the inspiration received, learning and ideas are generated. My counsel for churches in the beginning stages of a healing ministry is not to carbon copy a congregational worship style that is radically different from your own. Begin with the familiar. Design a basic liturgy that can be understood and accepted by the participants, many of whom will never have been in a public healing service.

I have attended healing services with and without anointing oil, with and without a sermon, with and without special music. Some healing services are thirty minutes in length, others continue for two or three hours. Some incorporate clergy-lay prayer teams, others only have clergy in leadership roles. Some ministers when praying with people lay their hands on two persons' heads at once, offering a very brief but sincere prayer for healing; others pray with one person at a time, taking as much time as they feel is needed. Some churches use a printed worship folder that is almost a replica of the Sunday morning liturgy with the addition of an invitation to come forward for healing prayers. Other congregations prefer no printed order of service and are more comfortable with an informal setting, having the worship leader announce what comes next.

It is always appropriate, especially in the beginning stages of a public healing ministry, to take time to explain to the gathered body what you are doing and why you are doing it. This teaching time can be part of the opening greeting or inserted as a brief introduction to each component of the liturgy. The goal is to put the worshipers "at-ease" and not to foster "dis-ease" in the healing environment.

Begin with the familiar in designing and writing liturgies for public healing services. You will discover many ways of enabling people to come into the presence, the light, and the love of the healing Christ.

Several liturgies for public healing services have been printed in Appendix A. All of these are presently being employed in various church settings. You will notice variety as well as common worship components. The question is: What liturgical design is acceptable in my local church? One way to test that is to design more than one, use them several weeks, then ask the participants to evaluate. A simple questionnaire might be worded:

1. What parts of the healing service do you find most helpful?
2. What parts do you not understand and would like to have explained?
3. What are some things you would like to change or have done differently in the healing service?
4. How has participation in the healing services helped you? Please share that in a sentence or two.

Whatever the liturgical setting in a public healing service, the mood must be one of sincere worship and prayerful expectancy. Responsible leadership helps each worshiper be aware of God's love, acceptance, forgiveness, pardon, healing, joy, and salvation in Jesus Christ. The physical environment of the room, the attitude of the gathered community, the leadership style of the liturgists, the design and flow of the order of service are significant factors in facilitating the healing process. Ample opportunity should always be given for personal meditation. Persons privileged to lead healing services are not putting on a performance for the congregation; rather, they are offering themselves in an act of love and obedience to Jesus Christ. They are conduits through which the Lord of the church brings his wholeness, health, and salvation. When we come intentionally into the presence of the healing Christ with receptivity, openness and faith, we allow him to minister to us at the point of our particular need of the moment in our lifelong journey toward wholeness.

Attention needs to be given to frequency, location, and time of the healing service. Even though many churches hold healing services monthly and semi-monthly, I strongly advocate weekly services for these reasons:

1. Monthly healing services tend to communicate a negative message about healing: "Healing services are not as important as weekly choir practice, church school, and Sunday morning services."

2. It is too difficult for many people to remember meetings that are held only on certain weeks and not on other weeks of the month.

3. Personal problems, tragedies, and dilemmas cannot always wait for the next monthly healing service and need to be dealt with as soon as possible. When engaged in private counseling, I often say to the Christian counselee, "Perhaps you have heard about our weekly services of Holy Communion and healing. I invite you to try to come to the next one. This could be a very effective form of spiritual therapy for you."

Ideally, the healing services should be held in the sanctuary or chapel. Here the worshipers are automatically surrounded by symbols of the faith that point beyond themselves to the Christ we love and serve. However, many churches do not have chapels, and the sanctuary often seems too large for the smaller numbers of persons who attend healing services. Be flexible and creative. One church which does not have a chapel holds its weekly services of Holy Communion and healing in the chancel area of the sanctuary. This was facilitated by taking out the screws that held the choir pews to the floor and placing the pews in a circular pattern with the focus being on the altar-communion table. Recently that same church converted an unused classroom into a lovely chapel setting.

It is best to keep the time, day, and location constant throughout the experimental phase. No certain hour or day of the week will suit everyone. If a change of time or day is necessary, give it an adequate test, keeping in mind that people are slow in adapting their personal schedules to church schedules.

Attendance at the weekly healing services often falls below the expectations of the persons in charge. You will find yourself quoting Jesus frequently, "Where two or three are gathered in my name, there am I in the midst of them" (Matt. 18:20). In congregations of several thousand members, the average attendance at the healing services may only be in the dozens. Our goal is to be faithful and obedient in offering a regular, well-publicized time for interested persons to participate in spiritual healing opportunities. Remember, our Lord can use the faith, love, compassion, and prayers of a few to feed the multitude.

There have been rare occasions (usually extremely bad weather) when I was the only one who showed up for the healing service. Not only did I have a beautiful time of personal communion with the Lord, but I was able to lift up intercessions on behalf of many persons who had turned in prayer requests earlier in the week. Do not become overly concerned with attendance figures. Do be faithful throughout the experiment. Then, based on what happened, be willing to modify, adapt, change, and try different approaches to accomplish the same goal.

As stated earlier, involvement of the laity is crucial, not only in building a support base within the congregation, but also in communicating the concept that leadership in the healing ministry is the responsibility of both clergy and laity. With the exception of presiding at the sacrament of Holy Communion, the laity in most denominations are permitted to be worship leaders and liturgists. After a year or so of attending weekly healing services, certain lay persons begin to emerge as potential leaders. Those who are motivated and receptive are the ones to be invited to take additional responsibilities. Many will hesitate, not having had previous experience. Here is where the enabling gifts of a loving pastor are so important. When the pastor invites lay persons to take leadership roles, support and practical help must accompany the invitation. Some lay persons feel more comfortable working behind the scenes, preparing the communion elements, setting up the worship center, arranging the furniture and other necessary details. Others, when given the opportunity, enjoy designing and leading the liturgy.[3]

An indispensable function that all lay persons can fulfill is to pray. Encourage churchwide prayer support for the healing ministry. Urge all church members to be in prayer at the time of the weekly services, even though they cannot be present. You will discover some lay persons in regular attendance who will not volunteer to be

---

3. Notice in some of the Liturgies for Public Healing Services (see Appendix A) an entry in the liturgy called *Commissioning of the Praying Teams.* This consists of having the praying team or teams kneel at the altar, immediately preceding the sacrament of Holy Communion, to be anointed with oil and to receive the laying-on-of-hands with this word:
   "In the name of God, the Father, the Son, and the Holy Spirit, we commission you to be an instrument of Christ's healing love. Amen."

up front leading the liturgy, but who will sit quietly and devotionally in the pews, faithfully praying and offering their prayers in faith and love. Prayer is the most significant work of the church. Without prayer, a spiritual healing ministry will never be effective. With prayer, possibilities are unlimited. Think of prayer, not as changing the mind of God; rather, as cooperating with God's highest will for our health, salvation, and wholeness.

Our role in praying with people and for people is to be the Lord's channel, conduit, catalyst, instrument for his healing love. The traditional prayer liturgy suggests that we pray to God the Father, through the Son, in the Holy Spirit. However, some Christians simply begin by addressing Jesus in their prayers.

Suggestions for healing prayer:

1. Be brief. Long and loud prayers are unnecessary. Keep them private and personal.
2. Be flexible. Be open to the leading of the Holy Spirit. Do not get locked in to a rigid prayer formula.
3. Be aware that the Lord of life already knows the details of the problem or situation. It is not necessary to rehearse them to him.
4. Be intentional in your act of faith and trust, lifting up each person into the light and love of the healing Christ.

Recommended prayer patterns when praying with people:

1. These hands are laid upon you in the name of the Father, the Son, and the Holy Spirit. May the power of his indwelling presence heal you of all infirmities of mind, body, and spirit, that you may serve him with a loving heart. Amen.
2. Lord Jesus Christ, strengthen and heal (name the person, if known). May thy healing love and healing power flow into his/her life. Banish all pain and sickness and sin. Give him/her the blessings of health in body, mind, and spirit. We ask these things and give

thee the glory in the name of the Father, the Son, and the Holy Spirit. Amen.
3. Thank you, Father, for this time of Holy Communion with you and with each other. We now lift up into your light and love (name the person, if known). Touch him/her. Bring him/her wholeness in body, mind, spirit, and relationships. For doing all of these things we thank you and give you the glory. Amen.

Our goal in praying with people is to concentrate on the presence of the healing Christ, to focus on the problem Solver, rather than on the problem. We want to cooperate with the love of God in the healing process. As Archbishop Richard C. Trench said, "We must not conceive prayer as an overcoming of God's reluctance, but a laying hold of his highest willingness."

Evaluation and Continuation

Imagine for a few moments that you are now into your third month of a three-month experimental healing ministry. You have learned some things. You have witnessed moments of amazing grace. You have made some mistakes. You now have to make some decisions about the future of the healing ministry in your church. You may want to use a questionnaire similar to this one in order to solicit reportable data for your church governing body.

QUESTIONNAIRE RELATED TO THE WEEKLY
HEALING SERVICES

1. I have attended regularly ____; occasionally ____; not once ____.
2. I think the services should be continued: ____yes; ____no.
3. I like the present time of the services: ____yes; ____no.

4. I could attend more often if these services were held at another time: ____yes; ____no.
5. Here are my suggestions for different times to hold these services:

6. The parts of the service I like the best are:
   a.
   b.
   c.
7. The parts of the service I like the least are:
   a.
   b.
   c.
8. I personally have been helped by this healing ministry:
   ____spiritually
   ____emotionally
   ____physically
   ____relationships with others
   ____other
9. Suggestions for improving the effectiveness of these services:

10. I am interested in attending a short-term study course or a one-day seminar dealing with an "in-depth" look at the spiritual healing ministry: ____yes; ____no.
11. Comments or questions:

Signature_____ (Optional)
Please return this to the church office by ____ (date).

Hopefully, you will get official sanction from your governing body to go ahead with another three to six months of intentional healing ministry. Keep in mind that any new form of ministry takes time to become established within the congregation. After several months of conducting public healing services, it is time to appoint a permanent, standing committee. The local church Healing Ministry Committee has at least five important tasks:

1. Be represented on the governing board and other
   · policymaking bodies of the church.
2. Be intentional about meeting with every organized group within the church to present information and answer questions about the weekly services of Holy Communion and Healing. This necessary educational process may not result in larger attendance at the services, but it will definitely clarify misunderstandings. It is also in order to invite each group and organization in the church to select a date to come together to one of the weekly services.
3. Be responsible for supervising and evaluating the healing ministry continuously, being sensitive to the total life and program of the church.
4. Be the sponsors for an annual spiritual healing mission in the church. This weekend event will bring in qualified persons who have had experience in an intentional healing ministry and who bring a fresh, dynamic, helpful voice.
5. Be aware of workshops, seminars, and conferences on spiritual healing offered in other places, encouraging interested church members to attend these educational and inspirational events.

Funding for a spiritual healing ministry in the local church can come through the church operating budget; however, experience shows that free-will offerings taken at the weekly services and the annual healing mission are usually more than sufficient to offset related expenses.

Finally, a word to the overly cautious. Some churches never get around to beginning an intentional healing ministry because:
1. They first want to study it thoroughly.
2. They want more time to think about it and pray about it.
3. They want to witness a miraculous healing within the congregation as a sign from the Lord to begin.
4. They want to be assured that someone in the church has been given the gift of healing.
5. They want to avoid all criticism and negative comments.

Analysis-paralysis is a disease that continues to afflict the institutional church. Whereas, the Lord of the church calls for boldness and willingness to take risks for him. Again, an ounce of obedience is worth a ton of Bible study.

In the beginning as well as in the week-by-week continuation of a healing ministry, be bold, be experimental, be faithful, be open to evaluation, be flexible. A willing pastor and a few ready-to-begin lay persons are all the Holy Spirit needs to reveal and to demonstrate the healing love and victorious power of Jesus Christ.[4]

GROUP STUDY GUIDE: CHAPTER 4

Preparation:
Locate area churches which have healing services.
In advance of the group Bible study, someone should consult two or three Bible commentaries to research the historical context of James 5:13-16.

---

4. For additional guidelines and practical suggestions, I highly recommend three sixty-six page booklets written by Don Bartow: *Beginning the Ministry of Healing, The Healing Service, The Healing Mission,* published in 1974 by Life Enrichment Publishers, Box 526, D. T. Station, Canton, Ohio 44701.

Materials needed for each participant for this session:
Paper and pencil
Church bulletins from last Sunday's service
Bibles
Chalk and chalkboard

1. CHRISTIAN WORSHIP AND HEALING
   Because all Christian worship is beneficial and helpful, why have special services of healing?
   Group Exercise
   Participants should each have a Sunday church bulletin. As a group, do the following:
   Step 1. Look at each part or section of the liturgy of
   worship and answer this question:"What was intended to happen that could have been beneficial and
   helpful to the worshipers?" Write on the chalkboard
   as many "positive intentions" as are suggested by
   the group.
   Step 2. How did anyone in the group who attended
   last Sunday morning's worship service experience
   the healing of body, mind, spirit, or relationships?
   Step 3. Take two or three minutes to review sections
   in Chapter 3 on "anointing with oil" and "laying-on-
   of-hands." Then discuss this question: What about
   the possibility of incorporating the opportunity for
   anointing with oil and laying-on-of-hands with
   prayers for healing within the regular Sunday morning worship service?
   Step 4. How do you react to the possibility of your
   church conducting weekly healing services at times
   other than Sunday mornings? Be realistic in your
   findings. If your conclusions are positive, list four
   action goals to accomplish a beginning and write
   them on the chalkboard.
2. VISITING, OBSERVING, PARTICIPATING IN
   PUBLIC HEALING SERVICES AT OTHER
   CHURCHES

Group Exercise

Make plans for a "field trip" to another church that conducts public healing services.

Can you think of persons not in your group who might like to go along? (If no churches with healing services are available, omit and proceed to the next exercise.)

3. BIBLE STUDY ON JAMES 5:13-16

This is a key passage revealing a New Testament teaching and practice on healing.

Group Exercise

a. Ask the person who consulted the Bible commentary to share his/her notes. Take no more than five to seven minutes for this background introduction.

b. Next, each person in the group read James 5:13-16 silently, making notes on these questions:

1. What did this say to the first Christians who read it in the early church?
2. What does this say to the church today?
3. What questions do I have about this passage?
4. What insights have I discovered here?

c. Bring all this to focus on this question: What does this passage tell us to do? (Write the findings on the chalkboard.)

4. CLOSING PRAYER TIME

As you prepare to close the meeting, read the action items written on the chalkboard. With this data, pray about goals and plans for the ministry of healing in your church. *Note:* If listed goals are not significant, let that fact become a matter of prayer.

5
WHEN HEALINGS DO NOT HAPPEN

Having this ministry by the mercy of God, we do not lose
heart.   2 Corinthians 4:1

A true story was told to me about a fifty-five-year-
old school teacher who had a stroke, resulting in speech
impairment and one slightly paralyzed leg. This woman
for years and years had sent a little money now and then
to a big-name faith healer from out-of-state, who in turn
sent her letters regularly. "Now," she thought to herself, "because I truly need healing for myself, I will send
him $1,000 and ask him to heal me." She did this and
promptly received an invitation to come to one of his
healing services where he would pray for her. So her
understanding and loving husband bundled her up in the
car and off they drove, several hundreds of miles.

At the healing service, she was sitting in the center
aisle in her wheelchair. After the sermon, the preacher
came down from the platform, stopped at her spot, put
his hands on her head, and prayed. Then he moved on
and prayed with others. Nothing happened that moment, that night, or the next day. She and her husband
went home disappointed.

The woman's mother, anxious to know what happened, said to her daughter, "Did you feel anything
special when the preacher laid his hands on your head
and prayed?" "No, nothing." "Did you have an inner
voice tell you to get up out of your wheelchair and
walk?" "No." "Well, something was not right, and the
only thing I know is that you didn't have enough faith."

A few weeks later she had another stroke, this one much more severe, and she died. At the funeral home, well-meaning friends tried to comfort the family by saying, "Shouldn't ever trust faith healers. Besides, it was God's will that your wife be taken from you."

This incident illustrates precisely why many Christians (especially clergy) remain aloof from personal involvement in anything that smacks of spiritual healing. Incorrect concepts are perpetuated when healing is related primarily to instantaneous, dramatic, physical healings which are dependent upon the amount of faith exhibited by the sick person. Then, to add insult to injury, the would-be comforters lay the blame on God with an escape-clause theology covering everything unexplainable, "It was God's will."

The purpose of this chapter is not to attempt an explanation of why the woman was not healed physically. Rather, it is to create a broader understanding about the complex nature of human illness and about some of the factors related to enjoying good health and living with poor health.

I believe God's will for the woman in the story was for her to recover from her stroke and to resume her teaching profession. Apparently, however, God's desire for her recovery was thwarted, as in too many tragic situations.

When healings do not happen in the exact manner anticipated by the doctor or the patient, the focus is usually on the physical. Yet, when one begins to comprehend what spiritual healing really is and does, the statement, "There are no failures," takes on credibility. Human beings are more than physical entities. The spiritual and mental dimensions of each person are constantly interacting with the physical. Yet, when we speak of miracles happening, we rarely assign that phenomenon to anything except the physical.

Don Bartow discusses the complex needs of the man who comes to a healing service in the church requesting anointing with oil and the laying-on-of-hands with prayer for his diagnosed terminal cancer. This man is not only a cancer patient, but he is also a person with a multitude of problems. When this man kneels at the altar for prayer to cure his cancer, he may also bring with him, consciously or unconsciously, fear of death, financial worries, concern for his family, guilt of past sins and present doubts, despair as he questions, "Why me?" fear of losing his job, almost unbearable pain, and physical and mental exhaustion.[1]

The prayers for healing offered in faith and cooperation with the man's prayers will prove to be beneficial. He may not be cured of the cancer, but may yet receive help in one or more of the other areas of his life. This is not to say that he will not be healed; he might be. The point is, when a person comes for healing he or she is always helped in some way.

This approach brings spiritual healing into proper focus. Granted, there are physical healings beyond explanation (miracles), but just as miraculous are the healings of the mind, the emotions, the spirit, family relations, financial difficulties, and human relationships. No one can ever say upon receiving the ministry of spiritual healing, "Nothing happened." Christ blesses and helps everyone who comes to him with a receptive mind, a loving heart, a willing spirit, and a prayer of faith. He stands by his promise, "I came that they may have life, and have it abundantly" (John 10:10).

Emily Gardner Neal gives perspective to this question of failure.

No one who properly understands spiritual healing ever turns from God because he is not healed, for no one who turns to Him in faith remains unhealed spiritually. Further, no one who

---

1. Don Bartow, "There Are No Failures," *The Adventures of Healing,* May, 1971, Article 13. Address: Life Enrichment Publishers, P.O. Box 526, Canton, Ohio 44701.

has experienced a healing of the spirit would exchange what he has received for a purely physical cure.[2]

The human experience of sickness and suffering cannot be simplistically explained; likewise, the experience of healing is often incomprehensible. The mystery of it, however, must not keep us from further research and experimentation in our common quest for wholeness.

Christians who take prayer seriously soon discover that prayer, far from being the last resort, is our first line of therapy. Praying for one another, praying with one another, praying because we love one another, is one of the primary ministries of every Christian. Yet there is a mystery about it all. We simply do not know why some persons get better and some do not. Our role, out of obedience to Jesus Christ, is to keep cooperating with God's highest will for wholeness, health, and salvation. Praying faithfully, researching diligently, and generously sharing our insights help us discover answers to the unanswered questions.

I am indebted to several Christians who, through their books on this subject, have shared their experiences in dealing with factors that hinder healing. I have made a list of helpful insights. In the three lists that follow, there are some duplication and some issues that may need clarification. The lists are by no means exhaustive. Those who want to do further study need to read these books for themselves and join the ranks of Christ's followers who not only want to learn more, but who also want to be effective instruments of his healing love.

In the book *Rediscovering the Gift of Healing* by Lawrence W. Althouse, a United Methodist minister, eight factors are listed in response to the question, "Why isn't everyone healed?"[3]

2. Emily Gardner Neal, *The Lord Is Our Healer* (Englewood Cliffs, New Jersey: Prentice-Hall, 1962), p. 56.
3. Lawrence W. Althouse, *Rediscovering the Gift of Healing* (Nashville: Abingdon, 1977), pp. 83-86.

1. People sometimes choose, consciously or unconsciously, to hold onto their illness.
2. People continue to surround themselves with the same influences that led them into illness.
3. [We have a] tendency to deal with symptoms rather than causes.
4. . . . Spiritual healing is not magic . . . . There is no waving of a magic wand to suspend the operation of the universe so that our own purposes may be served.
.5. Healing may be blocked or retarded when the patient is surrounded by an atmosphere that is unreceptive and hostile to healing. Through their negativity, people may greatly augment the destructive power of illness.
6. Sometimes we do not give God enough of ourselves with which to work.
7. Healing prayer may be ineffective because we are too specific and narrow in our receptivity, [and] we refuse to let God be God and determine how he will achieve his will in and through us.
8. Our failure to grasp that the healing of the physical body is not the highest of all goals.

Frances MacNutt, a Roman Catholic, in his book *Healing,* makes this observation, "God's normative will is that people will be healed, unless there is some countervailing reason. . . . To avoid simplistic approaches to healing we should be aware of the reasons people are not healed. In my ministry I have discovered at least eleven of these reasons and I imagine that there are several more that we will discover":

1. Lack of faith.
2. Redemptive suffering.
3. A false value attached to suffering.
4. Sin.
5. Not praying specifically.
6. Faulty diagnosis.
7. Refusal to see medicine as a way God heals.

8. Not using the natural means of preserving health.
9. Now is not the time.
10. A different person is to be the instrument of healing.
11. The social environment prevents healing from taking place.[4]

Dr. Frank B. Stanger, president of Asbury Theological Seminary in Wilmore, Kentucky, in his book, *God's Healing Community,* has an insightful chapter titled, "What Hinders Healing?" Having had an intentional healing ministry for more than a quarter of a century, he writes out of his experience:

Among the myths that have developed in relation to the failure to be healed are two common misconceptions: that such a failure is sometimes the sure evidence of a lack of faith on the part of the one seeking healing, and that on other occasions such failure is related to the will of God who does not purpose that a certain person be healed. We must disabuse our minds at once of these myths and the false assumptions upon which they are based.[5]

Dr. Stanger then goes on to discuss ten hindrances to healing found in the volume, *God's Healing Power,* by the late Edgar L. Sanford, and adds one more for a total of eleven.
1. The negativism of the secular world.
2. The negativism of the Christian world.
3. The negative influence of others.
4. Environmental confusion.
5. The absence of proper spiritual motivation.
6. The absence of compassion (Stanger's addition).
7. Discouragement.
8. The absence of anticipatory faith.

---

4. Francis MacNutt, *Healing* (Notre Dame, Indiana: Ave Maria, 1974), pp. 248-261.
5. Frank B. Stanger, *God's Healing Community* (Nashville: Abingdon, 1978), pp. 104-111.

9. The continuance of the factors that caused the illness
in the first place.
10. Old age.
11. Certain unknown factors.

In my experiences in this ministry, I have seen evi-
dences of all these hindrances to healing.

I would like to add a personal word. When Althouse
says, "People sometimes choose, consciously or unconsciously, to hold on to their illness,"[6] I am reminded of
Jesus' surgical question to the man who had been ill for
thirty-eight years, "Do you want to be healed?" (John
5:6).

This man, according to the story, did not realize it was
Jesus speaking to him and did not answer the question.
Instead, he offered the excuse, "Sir, I have no man to
put me into the pool when the water is troubled" (John
5:7).

Surely there are persons within your sphere of acquaintances who "enjoy poor health," who, although
they may not like being sick, definitely relish the attention, the pity, the excuse-making game.

A casual reading of the episode by the Pool of Be-
thesda might cause one to feel Jesus' question is out of
order. Yet, considering the man's thirty-eight years of
discouragement and hopelessness, Jesus had to say
something to arouse a positive attitude along with an
expectant hope.

John Sutherland Bonnell comments:

If one were addressing a group meeting of Alcoholics Anony-
mous, it would be unnecessary to explain the importance of
these words: "Do you want to be healed?" These people who
have battled through to self-discipline and self-control are
keenly aware of the significance of the question. I recall some
years ago asking Bill W., co-founder of A.A., "How would you
deal with a man who kept asserting: 'Don't worry about me; I
can handle this myself'?" Bill replied, "The most important

---

6. Althouse, *Rediscovering*, p. 83.

question we ask any candidate is, 'Do you really want sobriety?' 'Are you ready to stop drinking?' 'Do you want to be in command of yourself and your situation?' " "And what if he declines?" I asked him. "Well," said Bill, "we just have to let him go in the hope that when John Barleycorn kindles a still hotter fire under him, he'll be back to take the necessary steps."

Concludes Bonnell, "No one has yet explored to the deepest level such potent factors in recovery from illness as faith, expectation, and hope. No reputable surgeon would dream of operating on a patient who had surrendered to a 'death obsession.' It would be a losing fight."[7]

In MacNutt's list of eleven hindrances to healing, number one is LACK OF FAITH.[8] This needs a further word of clarification. Expectant faith, confident faith, trusting faith, childlike faith in the healing Christ must be present — somewhere. For instance, in a public healing service, this faith requisite may not always be residing in the persons requesting prayer for healing, nor may faith be present in the absentee persons for whom intercessory prayers are offered. Not only is it cruel, but also unnecessary to say to anyone, "The reason you were not healed is because you didn't have enough faith."

The faith required may be that of the liturgist or the praying team or within those who pray quietly in the pews or within those who cannot attend the public healing service, but are praying at that hour wherever they may be. As a Christian grows spiritually, he or she simultaneously grows in faith. I believe this means not so much in quantity, but rather in quality. When a Christian says, "I certainly have more faith now than I had ten years ago," I interpret that to mean, "I have more confidence and more trust in the supreme object of my faith (Jesus Christ) than I had ten years ago." Conversely,

7. John Sutherland Bonnell, *Do You Want to Be Healed?* (New York: Harper & Row, Publishers, 1968), pp. 85-86.
8. MacNutt, *Healing,* p. 249

when a person says, "I seem to have lost my faith," I hear, "I need to get in touch again with Jesus Christ."

Although it is true that Jesus did help and heal persons whose faith was unknown and unquestioned, the miracles were too numerous to count when the people came to him in faith, confidently expecting something good to happen in their lives.

One more personal comment, this one related to Stanger's list, number six, THE ABSENCE OF COMPASSION. This is definitely addressed to everyone who presently has leadership roles in an intentional healing ministry. To quote Stanger, "Healing power cannot flow where compassion is lacking."[9] In the healing ministry we are dealing with human beings at their most sensitive and vulnerable levels of existence, a ministry never to be taken lightly or routinely. Because those who minister (lay and clergy alike) are also vulnerable, tempted, and limited in many ways, a personal reliance on the Holy Spirit is a necessity. A personal dependence on the Holy Spirit is mandatory for the most effective results. All those leading in the healing ministry must be open, compassionate, forgiving channels of God's redeeming and healing love.

Seeing people through the eyes of Christ will prevent us from using the healing ministry for personal gain and glory. Before asking the question, "Do I have the gift of healing?" ask yourself, "Am I a loving person?" "Do I really care about other people?" "When I look upon those who are hurting, wounded, struggling, suffering, do I experience compassion within me?"

Consider seriously these two related statements:

First, all physical healing is temporary at best.

Even when the dramatic, healing miracle occurs, it is only a matter of time before there will be another malfunction or breakdown of the human body's physical systems. The Creator has not designed or programmed

---

9. Stanger, *Community*, p. 109.

the body to last forever. The healthiest people in the world eventually die. This is not to build a case for a quick, fatalistic acceptance of our illnesses and accidents; rather, to plead for a larger perspective of one's physical well-being and to seek actively the abundant, healthy life God intends for every human being until the moment of physical death.

Secondly, physical death is not the end but the transition to a new chapter in the life of every Christian.

In the context of the Christian faith, death is sometimes called the threshold to ultimate healing. As Paul puts it, when speaking about the resurrection of the body after it is dead and buried:

What is sown is perishable, what is raised is imperishable. It is sown in dishonor, it is raised in glory. It is sown in weakness, it is raised in power. It is sown a physical body, it is raised a spiritual body (1 Cor. 15:42-44).
Flesh and blood cannot inherit the kingdom of God, nor does the perishable inherit the imperishable. Lo! I tell you a mystery. We shall not all sleep, but we shall all be changed. . . . For this perishable nature must put on . . . immortality. . . . "Death is swallowed up in victory." . . . Thanks be to God, who gives us the victory through our Lord Jesus Christ (1 Cor. 15:50-51, 53-54, 57).

Although death, in the minds of many people, is the ultimate tragedy, Christians are heirs of the resurrection of Jesus Christ. This is not to make excuses for what we often perceive as failure in healing before death, or to make slight the deep pain in grieving over the loss of a loved one. This is not to be insensitive to natural fear and ambivalent feelings about the moment of death or the process of dying. Rather, this is an affirmation that only through death and dying can we realize the complete wholeness for which we were created. A person who has had to struggle through life with crippling arthritis, loss of vision, the burden of brain damage, amputation, or other handicaps may only be fully healed through that transition from life on earth to life in a different state of existence.

According to the New Testament, eternal life begins the moment a person consciously and intentionally accepts Jesus Christ and believes in him without reservation as Lord and Savior. Death of the body, then, becomes an event within ongoing, eternal life (see John 3:16-17; 10:10; 11:25-27). For this reason, we pray for a person's healing even in the face of death, cooperating with God's will for wholeness on both sides of death.

Christians—the resurrection people—would do well to recite frequently this benediction from the Roman liturgy:

In him, who rose from the dead,
  our hope of resurrection dawned.
The sadness of death gives way
  to the bright promise of immortality.
Lord, for your faithful people
  life is changed, not ended.[10]

GROUP STUDY GUIDE: CHAPTER 5

Materials needed by each participant for this session:
  Four 3x5 cards
  Pencils
1. THERE ARE NO FAILURES
  Christ blesses and helps everyone who comes to him with a receptive mind, a loving heart, a willing spirit, and a prayer of faith.
  Group Exercise
  Has anyone in the group ever had the experience of praying for a certain healing but receiving a different kind of healing? If so—
  How did that leave you feeling?
  How do you feel about it now?
2. HINDRANCES TO HEALING
  Three lists of hindrances to healing are listed from

10.From Preface I in the Mass of the Dead, *The Sacramentary of the Roman Missal* (New York: Catholic Book Publishing Company, 1974), p. 527.

the writings of Lawrence Althouse, Francis Mac-Nutt, and Frank Stanger.

Group Exercise

a. Take two minutes to review these lists on pages 68-70.

b. What additional hindrances are not listed? (List on the chalkboard.)

c. What should be the Christian's attitude and actions toward persons who seem to "enjoy poor health"?

3. DO YOU WANT TO BE HEALED?

This question Jesus asked the man who had been ill for thirty-eight years.

Group Exercise

Distribute Bibles to each group member.

Everyone read John 5:1-18. What hindrances might Jesus have had in mind that needed to be overcome when he asked: "Do you want to be healed?"

4. THE ROLE OF FAITH

The author interprets faith in terms of quality rather than quantity.

Group Exercise

Has anyone had the experience of being prayed for without knowing it at the time? If so, describe the outcome.

5. PHYSICAL DEATH IS NOT THE END BUT THE TRANSITION TO A NEW CHAPTER IN THE LIFE OF EVERY CHRISTIAN.

This statement is related to another: "All physical healing is temporary at best."

Group Exercise

From the context of the two statements above, discuss the following: "Only through death and dying can we realize the complete wholeness for which we were created."

6. INTERCESSORY PRAYER

"Prayer is not the least but the most we can do for another human being."

Group Exercise
a. Distribute one 3x5 card and a pencil to each participant.
b. Think of three persons within your sphere of acquaintance who seem to have hindrances to their healings and write one name on each card.
c. In a period of worship and prayer each of you read the names on your card to the group, adding at the end, "I lift each one into the light and love of Jesus and thank him for the healing that has begun. Amen."

7. PRAYING FOR OUR PERSONAL NEEDS
Everyone has personal needs. It is OK to pray (petition) for ourselves.

Group Exercise
a. Distribute one 3x5 card to each participant.
b. Write three of your personal needs of healing on the card.
c. Consider hindrances and write them (if any) on the card.
d. In a moment of worship and prayer in silence, lift up in prayer your personal needs (and hindrances to healing, if any) written on the card.

8. HOMEWORK
a. Enter a covenant to take home the intercessory prayer cards and the personal petition prayer cards, lifting up in prayer each day the written concerns.
b. Bring the cards with you to the next group meeting, sharing any help in healing you are able to report.

6

FORGIVENESS IS A KEY TO GOOD HEALTH

Lord, how often shall my brother sin against me, and I forgive him?   Matthew 18:21

Apart from the urgency of having healing services in the church and the practical procedures which make the healing ministry possible, there are two additional matters which require attention. The first is the intrinsic power of forgiveness in healing (chapter 6); the second is the relationship which spiritual healing services have to the charismatic movement (chapter 7).

Forgiveness is popularly accepted as a spiritual principle which was clearly taught, illustrated, and practiced by Jesus. Forgiveness is universally respected in promoting harmonious social relationships. How many people, however, look upon forgiveness as a crucial key to personal good health? How many realize unforgiveness is a major contributor to unhealthiness? Not only is forgiveness good for one's soul and one's social life, it is equally good medicine for one's physical and mental well-being.

The Bible consistently witnesses to the beneficial influences of forgiveness. Contemporary Christian leaders in the healing ministry underscore the benefits of forgiveness. Medical research is also adding new insights to the causative relationship between negative emotions, stress, and poor health.

Have you ever heard someone say, "That man gives me a pain in the neck!" Or, "I can't stand to be in the same room with her. She makes me sick to my stomach!" They are likely telling it like it is.

Examine some of your own emotional patterns. Have you ever been so upset with someone you could not eat? Have you ever been so angry you could not sleep? Have you ever been in an argument and a few hours later gone to bed because of a headache that would not quit?

Psalm 32 could have been written by many burdened and bound-up people living today:

When I declared not my sin, my body wasted away
    through my groaning all day long.
For day and night thy hand was heavy upon me;
    my strength was dried up as by the heat of summer
    (vv. 3-4).

We recognize the psalmist's description of guilt's influence on body and mind. We can fill in the details: He cannot eat, cannot relax, cannot sleep. He is losing weight, has no energy, no ambition. He is emotionally drained. The picture of "a nervous wreck." Although he does not name his undeclared sin, experience proves that sin by any name can exert harmful effects on the sinner. We could insert these possible names of sins whose cumulative influence is truly disastrous: resentment, bitterness, revenge, jealousy, unforgiveness.

Notice the very next verse (v. 5) of Psalm 32:

I acknowledged my sin to thee,
    and I did not hide my iniquity;
I said, "I will confess my transgressions to the Lord";
    then thou didst forgive the guilt of my sin.

Release and help came only after he was willing to admit he needed forgiveness. The Lord answered his plea and erased the guilt of his sin. Knowing that this is the way the Lord operates, what prevents us from admitting our guilt, confessing our sin, and allowing God to forgive us? The answer to that question comes in verse 9. After the psalmist shares his personal anguish followed by his new sense of freedom through forgiveness, he writes: "Be not like a horse or a mule, without understanding." We compound our problems when we are not willing to admit we have a problem. Call it stubbornness, bull-headedness, or personal pride. No matter! Unforgiveness is not Christian; nor is it healthy!

Recall that Sunday afternoon in September of 1974 when President Gerald Ford returned to the White House in Washington, D.C., after worshiping at St. John's Episcopal Church fresh from partaking of the bread and the cup in the sacrament of Holy Communion. Across the news media came the announcement of President Ford's pardon of Richard Nixon. I read the following statement in *Time* magazine concerning the event.

Each of us is to a degree lost, tied to the rest of humanity — and to God — by fragile strands of grace, strands that fray and break. Pardon is a favor that we may sometimes be in a position to grant, but more importantly, it is one that we will always need.[1]

Jesus repeatedly emphasized that his followers are to be forgiving people. Christians are to take seriously his words, "Be merciful, even as your Father is merciful" (Luke 6:36). Another dimension of forgiveness is recorded in Luke:

If your brother sins, rebuke him (reprimand him), and if he repents (if he is truly sorry), forgive him; and if he sins against you seven times in a day, and turns to you seven times and says, "I repent," you must forgive him (17:3-4).

Would any of us put up with someone who sinned against us seven times in one day? Some people draw the line at one, two, or maybe three at the most. When Jesus uses the number seven, he is holding up a figure that pushes the limits of toleration. Seven times in one

---

1. "The Theology of Forgiveness," *Time*, September 23, 1974, p. 36.

day really means unlimited pardons. Notice Jesus also says, "You must forgive him." Have you ever asked someone to forgive you, knowing that you were in the wrong, only to have that person say, "Go away, I don't want to talk about it." Or some other remark that came out meaning, "I'm not going to accept your forgiveness"? Jesus says we have no choice in the matter. When someone comes to us asking forgiveness, we must forgive.

Some people apparently took the number seven literally and interpreted the eighth offense as not requiring forgiveness. Another problem all of us face is what to do with those people who hurt us, who sin against us, but who never get around to apologizing. Jesus dealt with both these issues in Matthew.

Then Peter came up and said to him [Jesus], "Lord, how often shall my brother sin against me, and I forgive him? As many as seven times?" Jesus said to him, "I do not say to you seven times, but seventy times seven" (18:21-22).

Seventy times seven. Even if taken literally, this would multiply out to 490 times. By then, the forgiver would be in the habit of forgiving. But don't strain by taking it literally.

Here Jesus gives us an astronomical figure to say in a more dramatic way that love keeps no score and that forgiveness has nothing to do with arithmetic. Also, in this teaching Jesus omits that part, "If he repents, forgive him" (Luke 17:3), implying that our forgiveness of another human being is not dependent on that person "eating humble pie" and apologizing appropriately. What then is the basis of Christian forgiveness? Recall our Lord's prayer in his Sermon on the Mount. In Matthew 6:14-15, he adds a significant dimension:

For if you forgive men their trespasses, your heavenly Father also will forgive you; but if you do not forgive men their trespasses, neither will your heavenly Father forgive your trespasses.

Here is the spiritual foundation of Jesus' instructions to all his followers advocating a life-style of unlimited forgiveness. If we choose to be selective about whom we are going to forgive, whom we are not going to forgive, and how many times we are going to forgive, then we have imposed this same limitation and selectivity on our heavenly Father's forgiveness of us. Personally, I need all the mercy, grace, and forgiveness God has to give. Lack of forgiveness on my part not only impinges upon relationships at the human level, but also impedes my relationship with my heavenly Father.

Take note of one more instruction by Jesus on this crucial subject.

Therefore I tell you, whatever you ask in prayer, believe that you receive it, and you will. And whenever you stand praying, forgive, if you have anything against any one; so that your Father also who is in heaven may forgive you your trespasses (Mark 11 :24-25).

That other person may never offer that apology. That other person may never forgive us and be reconciled with us. In this scripture passage, Jesus puts it clearly: The burden is not on the other person, it is on the one doing the praying. We have no control over other people's attitudes and actions, but we are responsible for our own attitudes and actions. This quotation from Mark's Gospel also calls us to consider the relationship between prayer and forgiveness. If some of our prayers seem to be going nowhere, if some of our deepest petitions apparently remain unanswered, we would do well to look closely at all of our relationships. An unforgiving attitude, according to Jesus, is an unacceptable attitude in prayer, and it promotes dis-ease within. In her book *Healing Prayer*, Barbara Shlemon suggests:

It is good practice during prayer time to sit quietly and ask the Lord to bring to mind anyone whom we need to forgive. If a name comes to us we can ask the Holy Spirit to grant us the grace necessary to "see" this individual with the eyes of Jesus and to forgive him with the Lord's forgiving love. We can say a prayer of thanksgiving that Jesus will correct anything lacking in our human ability to love with His perfect love.[2]

Another area to explore continuously is our personal expectations of other people. There may be someone who has failed to meet your expectations: a father or a mother, a son or a daughter, a husband or a wife, a friend or a neighbor, a classmate or a colleague. You may even be upset with God for failing you in a time of great personal need. Possibly you are disappointed in yourself for failing to meet your own expectations of yourself. There are all those people—usually strangers —who treat us indifferently. Put that all together and it can spell *resentment.* Unresolved resentments create unforgiveness, and unforgiveness promotes unhealthiness.

Human relationships can become very complicated. Some people hurt us deeply with little sensitivity to our personal feelings. My Christian conscience tells me, "I know I should forgive and forget," while my stomach is saying, "No way am I going to do that." How do we get rid of these hurts, these insults, these bitter resentments?

Because of our human nature, we all need God's help with this area of our life. We cannot wait until we feel like forgiving someone before we forgive. In difficult situations, when you simply cannot bring yourself to forgive, ask this question, "Am I willing to *try to be willing* to forgive? Am I willing to let God soften my hardened, unbending, unforgiving attitude as a prelude to genuine forgiveness? "

Our heavenly Father honors that kind of honesty and does give us the willingness to forgive when we ask him. Remember that our emotions change slowly, much slower than the decision making processes of the mind. It is not

2. Barbara L. Shlemon, *Healing Prayer* (Notre Dame, Indiana: Ave Maria, 1976), pp. 58-59.

unusual for one's emotions to lag behind one's intellectual decisions. When studying the healing ministry of our Lord, it is clear that in certain healing situations the confession and forgiveness of sins were determining factors. John Sutherland Bonnell, Presbyterian minister and pioneer in the field of counseling and mental health, points out that "the healing of the soul is to be recognized as something even more important than the healing of the body. In some instances of our Lord's ministry these occur simultaneously. Whenever he said to those who came to him for healing, 'Thy sins are forgiven thee, go in peace,' we may be sure that the alienation from God within the life of the individual had first to be healed and his sins forgiven before he could receive the inner peace so sorely lacking."[3]

We note with focused interest the counsel to confession in the Book of James 5:15-16 regarding the healing ministry of the New Testament church:

If he has committed sins, he will be forgiven. Therefore confess your sins to one another, and pray for one another, that you may be healed.

All illness is not due to sin, but experience dictates the necessity of personal daily examination of consciences and the confession of sins. To be insensitive to this critical area of our lives is to overlook a crucial factor in our total well-being and good health.

Dr. Bonnell states, "A therapeutic force of great value to mankind is the received forgiveness of God. This is due to the fact that one of the root causes of most of the emotional maladjustments and psychosomatic illnesses in our civilization is an unrelieved sense of guilt."[4]

Medical researchers are adding new insights to the relationship between forgiveness and good health. Dr. Hans Selye, a Canadian medical doctor in Montreal, has done extensive research in the area of stress and dis-

---

3. Bonnell, *Healed*, p. 91.
4. Ibid., p. 92.

tress. Although his investigation is primarily in the science of biochemistry, he discovered serendipitously that positive emotions and attitudes (gratitude, thanksgiving, praise, forgiveness, joy) are health-enhancing factors. Conversely, negative emotions and attitudes (resentment, revenge, anger, hate, jealousy) have a debilitating and disease-inducing effect on the body.[5]

Another significant study published in 1962 was written by Dr. Loring T. Swaim, a physician. Dr. Loring T. Swaim has specialized for fifty years in the field of orthopedics, and for twenty years has been an instructor in arthritis at Harvard Medical School. This fascinating book is filled with well-documented, matter-of-fact case histories of Dr. Swaim's patients. Described within is what happened and what can happen when ordinary men and women, tangled in the intricate web of human nature and crippled by disease, are set free by the surrender of resentment and bitterness and the submission of self-will to God's will.

The author is convinced that emotional stress such as negative attitudes toward others can be causative of rheumatoid arthritis and other organic diseases. In addition to treating his patients with the latest medical and physical therapies, Dr. Swaim prescribed spiritual therapy to those who were receptive and willing.

He describes what he calls "spiritual laws," which lead to improved health and wholeness when obeyed.

The Law of Love (Matthew 22:39 and John 15:12)
The Law of Apology (Matthew 5:23-24)
The Law of Change (Matthew 7:5)
The Law Concerning Fault-finding (Matthew 7:1 and
    Matthew 7:12)
The Law of Forgiveness (Matthew 6:14)[6]

---

5. Recommended readings are two books by Hans Selye, *The Stress of Life* (New York: McGraw Hill, 1956), and *Stress Without Distress* (New York: J.B. Lippincott Company, 1974).
6. Loring T. Swaim, *Arthritis, Medicine and the Spiritual Laws* (New York: Chilton Company, 1962).

Not all his patients were open to applying these spiritual principles in their lives, but for those who did there was noticeable and often dramatic improvement in their condition.

Forgiveness is also at the heart of inner healing. Ruth Carter Stapleton defines inner healing as

a process of emotional reconstruction experienced under the guidance of the Holy Spirit. It is not an attempt to supplant psychiatry or to ignore the wisdom found in secular psychology. Historically the church has recognized Jesus Christ as the great physician; his message and Spirit have inspired the development of medical and psychiatric science as well as the spiritual exercise of praying for miraculous physical healing. Inner healing of emotional trauma is the logical, natural extension of this same inspiration.[7]

Inner healing is sometimes called "healing of the past," "healing of the negative emotions," or in Agnes Sanford's terms, "the healing of memories." The basic idea is this: Jesus Christ, who is the same today as he was yesterday and will be forever (Hebrews 13:8) is not bound by time and space as we are.

When we pray for inner healing, we are really asking Jesus to walk back into the dark places of our lives and bring healing to the distressing and painful memories of the past. We need to take Jesus into the areas of our unforgiveness toward those who have taught us to fear, hate, and reject. We need to take him (love) into the relationships where there was no love.[8]

Persons whose illnesses do not respond in positive ways to medicine and counseling and who seem to be bound up by painful events in their past are encouraged to try inner healing therapy. The goal of inner healing is to be set free, to be liberated from bondage to the painful past and to live fully in the present without fear of

7. Ruth Carter Stapleton, *The Experience of Inner Healing* (Waco, Texas: Word Books, Publishers, 1977), p. 9.
8. Ruth Carter Stapleton, *The Gift of Inner Healing* (Waco, Texas: Word Books, Publishers, 1976), p. 10.

the future. At the heart of inner healing is forgiveness — a key to good health. As in all matters of faith and practice, the Christian looks to Jesus, our supreme model and master teacher. By his personal example, Jesus demonstrated what it means to forgive whenever forgiveness is called for, whether or not we feel like forgiving. When he was dying on the cross, he did not wait until his enemies apologized! He did not wait until he was feeling good before he prayed, "Father, forgive them; for they know not what they do" (Luke 23:34).

If anyone had the right to be unforgiving, it was the innocent, crucified Jesus who died expressing forgiveness. Everyone who calls him Lord and who takes the name Christian, therefore, forfeits all rights and privileges to withhold forgiveness.

GROUP STUDY GUIDE: CHAPTER 6

Materials needed for this session:
    Bibles for each person
    Note paper and pencils
1. A BIBLE STUDY ON FORGIVENESS
    RESENTMENT, BITTERNESS, REVENGE, JEALOUSY, UNFORGIVENESS. . . .
    These are sins whose cumulative influence is disastrous to the body, mind, spirit, and all relationships.
    a. Divide yourselves into groups of three and distribute Bibles to each group.
    b. Each group should consider one or more of the following passages on forgiveness.
        Luke 6:36
        Matthew 5:7
        Luke 17:3-4
        Matthew 18:21-22
        Matthew 6:14-15
        Mark 11:24-25
    c. Allow ten minutes for the group to consider its

assigned passage(s) in light of this question: What does this teach us about forgiveness?

d. One person from each group briefly summarize the group's discoveries.

2. A BIBLE STUDY OF SPIRITUAL LAWS

The spiritual laws discovered by Dr. Loring T. Swaim (p. 84) are insights which deserve closer examination.

a. In the groups of three, study the following passages in the context of the particular designated law.

> The Law of Love (Matthew 22:39 and John 15:12)
>
> The Law of Apology (Matthew 5:23-24)
>
> The Law of Change (Matthew 7:5)
>
> The Law Concerning Fault-finding (Matthew 7:1; 7:12)
>
> The Law of Forgiveness (Matthew 6:14)

b. Ask one person from each group briefly to summarize the group's discoveries.

3. A REVIEW OF "FORGIVENESS: A KEY TO GOOD HEALTH"

As a group look back over chapter 6 and do these two things:

a. Verbalize the one big idea that spoke most directly to your personal situation.

b. Discuss the implication for your church of the relationship of forgiveness and the healing ministry.

4. PRAYING PRAYERS OF FORGIVENESS

Reading about forgiveness or even studying the Bible on the subject of forgiveness are no substitutes for prayers of forgiveness. The following prayer experience should be unhurried. Adjust the lights as needed. Prepare for an uninterrupted time of prayer.

Group Exercise

a. Get as comfortable as possible, breathing deeply,

relaxing your mind and body, being open and receptive to the Holy Spirit.

b. Someone should pray the following prayer aloud:

"We adore you, O Christ, we praise you, O Christ, because through your holy cross you have redeemed the world and saved each of us from our sins. Through your holy cross you have forgiven us and loved us even before we knew what forgiveness and love were all about. (Pause)

"Right now, O Christ, each one of us comes to you seeking help in being forgiving persons. (Pause)

"Some of us are having difficulty forgiving. We need your strength, and a willingness to be willing to forgive. Help each of us overcome our stubborness and pride that cripple us in so many ways. (Pause)

"And now, O Christ, in a conscious, deliberate act of our will we want to forgive everyone who has anything against any of us.

"Some of us need to forgive our parents. (Pause)

"Some of us need to forgive our children. (Pause)

"Some of us need to forgive God, our heavenly Father. (Pause)

"Some of us need to forgive ourselves. (Pause)

"Some of us need to forgive someone who died before we were reconciled. (Pause)

"Lord, hear our prayers as we pray specifically by name. Lord, I forgive _____(name). (Pause for personal prayers of forgiveness in silence.)

"Lord, we now turn over to you, ourselves and all those persons we have named in forgiveness. As you direct any of us to take tangible action, give us the will to follow through (it might be a phone call, a personal letter, an apology, or restitution).

"Gracious, merciful Lord, help each one of us know the joy of forgiveness, the joy of burdens taken away, the joy of new life in Christ, the joy of health and wholeness in body, mind, spirit, and in all relationships. In the name of the Father, the Son, and the Holy Spirit we pray and dedicate ourselves. Amen."

7
CHARISMA
WITHOUT CONFLICT

Make love your aim, and earnestly desire the spiritual gifts.
1 Corinthians 14:1

Spiritual healing services are not widely held in churches today. I suspect that most every congregation has at least some persons who favor enhancing the church's ministry at this vital point. One reason for hesitancy is confusion about what relationship spiritual healing services have with the so-called charismatic movement.

The word *charismatic* comes from the Greek word *charisma*, which can be translated "a divine gratuity," "a spiritual endowment," or "a free gift." The term *charismatic gifts* is used in a popular sense to identify the nine gifts *(charismata)* of the Spirit mentioned in 1 Corinthians 12:4-11: prophecy, healing, working miracles, tongues, interpretation of tongues, wisdom, knowledge, faith, discernment.

Other New Testament passages expand the gifting activity of the Holy Spirit to include the following: teaching, serving, exhortation, giving, giving aid, compassion (Rom. 12:6-8); apostleship, helps, administration, workers of miracles (1 Cor. 12:28); evangelism, shepherding (Eph. 4:11).

It is significant to note that "prophecy" is the only gift mentioned in all four of the passages. In Paul's opinion this is one of the gifts that is especially valuable (1 Cor. 14:1). The New Testament does not attempt to give an exhaustive inventory of the spiritual gifts. The gifting activity of the Holy Spirit is far more generous than the human mind can imagine.

Kenneth Kinghorn in his book, *Gifts of the Spirit*, suggests this definition:

A spiritual gift is a supernatural ability or capacity given by God to enable the Christian to minister and to serve.[1]

Kinghorn has five basic principles that can help all Christians better understand spiritual gifts:

1. God imparts spiritual gifts according to his divine grace; they cannot be earned through human merit.
2. God gives spiritual gifts according to his own discretion; God is not bound by man's wishes.
3. God wills that every Christian exercise spiritual gifts; these divine enablings are not limited to a few believers.
4. God provides gifts for the purpose of ministry and service; they are not given to draw attention to man or to satisfy his ego.
5. God intends that the ministry of the church be accomplished through spiritual gifts; human talents alone are not adequate for spiritual ministry.[2]

Jesus insisted that true character is revealed by the productive qualities of a person's life (see Matt. 7:15-20). Likewise, Paul taught that manifestations of the Holy Spirit's gifts are evidenced in certain "fruit of the Spirit," such as love, joy, peace, patience, kindness, goodness, faithfulness, gentleness, self-control (see Gal. 5:22-23). In his Letter to the Romans, Paul extends the list of Holy Spirit fruit to give us a composite picture of a Christian life-style (12:9-18).

---

1. Kenneth Kinghorn, *Gifts of the Spirit* (Nashville: Abingdon, 1976), p. 22.
2. Ibid., pp. 22-30.

What is the difference then between gifts of the Spirit and fruit of the Spirit? Kinghorn informs us, "Spiritual fruit has to do with our relationships and the spiritual quality of our lives. Spiritual gifts, on the other hand, have to do with our calling and our function in ministry. Spiritual fruit relates to what we *are*; spiritual gifts relate to what we *do*."[3]

It appears that no one Christian has ever had all of the spiritual gifts mentioned in the New Testament. All of the gifts are not for everyone, but all of the fruit is for every disciple of Jesus Christ.

The Holy Spirit, let it be restated, bestows his gifts for functional ministry and for the common good of the Christian community (the church). "For building up the body of Christ" is the statement in Ephesians 4:12. Why is it, then, that one of the Holy Spirit gifts, the gift of tongues, tends to be confusing, divisive, and misunderstood? The practice of speaking in tongues (glossolalia) occurred in certain churches during the first two and a half centuries of the Christian era. Then it seemed to disappear almost entirely from the Christian movement. From 1650 to 1900, speaking in tongues was sporadic. At the beginning of the twentieth century, it began to manifest itself more extensively than ever before and is connected with the birth of the Pentecostal movement in the United States.

In 1900, Charles F. Parham, a young Methodist minister, started the Bethel Bible College in Topeka, Kansas, teaching that "the Baptism of the Holy Spirit" must be accompanied by "speaking in tongues" as evidence. January 1, 1901, is called the birthday of the Pentecostal movement. On that day, Agnes Ozman, one of Parham's students, began to speak in tongues. Another student, W. J. Seymour, a black minister from Los Angeles, California, came to Parham seeking the baptism of the Holy Spirit. Seymour returned to Los Angeles after several

---

3. Ibid., p. 21.

months of study and prayer. There he led a revival that lasted for three years and launched the American Pentecostal movement.

During the past two decades, within main-line denominations, ministers and lay persons have been speaking in tongues and experiencing various gifts of the Spirit. This is sometimes called "neo-Pentecostalism" (the new Pentecostals).

The neo-Pentecostals differ from the classical Pentecostals in that they do not organize themselves into separate churches which are characterized by speaking in tongues. Another difference is that Pentecostals insist that an instantaneous sanctification experience known as "baptism of the Holy Spirit" must be confirmed by speaking in tongues. The new Pentecostals, or "charismatics," are divided on the importance of the gift of tongues. Some classify it as a lesser and minor gift; others believe all Christians should actively seek the gift of tongues.

Dr. Robert Tuttle, a United Methodist minister and author who describes himself as a charismatic who speaks in tongues, does not believe God intends this particular gift for all Christians, but only for those who need it. "Some of us are just not as articulate as others," he said, "and when the Holy Spirit speaks through us, tongues are the only way we can get it all out. Some people don't have that problem. Some don't need tongues."

Tuttle agrees with Dr. Albert Outler, a professor at the Perkins School of Theology in Dallas, who looks upon tongues the same way he views the expression of tears in the spiritual life; "It is a way for the overfilled to overflow."[4]

What, then, is the charismatic movement? It is one of the ways through which the Holy Spirit is renewing the

---

4. *United Methodist Reporter,* April 16, 1976.

church today. Actually, the church is a movement that will never stop moving or reforming. Charismatic experiences are spiritual renewal experiences within the larger context of the Christian movement.

We should support, keep, and use that which helps and heals the church. Let us discard and disregard that which divides and breeds dissension. A self-righteous or spiritually superior attitude on the part of any Christian (charismatic or non-charismatic) reveals that the Holy Spirit has yet to do his primary work in that Christian: namely, to direct him or her in the more excellent way—the way of love (1 Cor. 12:31—14:1).

This is precisely a notable rationale for a viable, flexible, intentional healing ministry within the church today. Wholeness, health, and salvation are God's gifts to all his people through Jesus Christ. I understand the healing ministry of all churches to be connected with the Holy Spirit's activity in our world today. Indeed, if the Holy Spirit pulled out, we might as well stay home. On the other hand, I do not see the necessity of all healing ministries being charismatic in the popular sense.

A healing ministry will be acceptable by a majority of Christians when it is sacramental in nature, emphasizing God's grace, love, and power within the obedient community of faith. My experience is that the healing ministry is a bridge of understanding, a common meeting ground for charismatics and non-charismatics, because it lifts up the love of God for all persons. When a person accepts Jesus Christ, he or she receives the gift of the Holy Spirit, and the Holy Spirit, in turn, begins to impart and endow that committed life with certain spiritual gifts (see Acts 2:38).

In one sense all Christians are charismatic, but not all Christians openly and actively acknowledge the power of the Holy Spirit at work in them. Not all Christians intentionally open their lives to receive more of the Holy Spirit's power and gifts as do the avowed charismatics or neo-Pentecostals.

The following statement written by the Reverend Kelly Silvers summarizes the tension and the promise of charismatic renewal in the life of the church:

The charismatic movement . . . can make a valuable contribution to the church, provided the concern for catholicity and the use of charismatic gifts for the edification of the Church stand tenaciously. If not, then it will inevitably be rejected by the Church, and may certainly produce a schism.

There is a real possibility for a rich blend in the unity of the Church, through the acceptance of the contribution of charismatics, and vice versa. If the central concern of both sides of the tension is to glorify Christ and carry out the mission in the world, then the point of common identification should limit the distractions to a minimum.

If each side of the tension becomes involved with a ruthless determination to insist on arguing over the points of difference, then it stands to reason that the issues which are emphasized will occupy the most attention—namely, the points of disagreement.

If there is to be any lasting unity in a Church which has always manifested the historical spirit-structure tension, certainly the key to the unity is not by emphasizing the differences to the point of mutual exclusion, but to emphasize that which should be common to all—the mandate to spread the Gospel of Jesus Christ to the world.

In this sense, as all look to Christ, it seems that the diversities could strengthen the Church, rather than weaken it.

Perhaps a subtle warning to the Church today might come from Galatians 5:14-15, "For the whole law is fulfilled in one word, 'You shall love your neighbor as yourself.' But if you bite and devour one another, take heed that you are not consumed by one another."[5]

This is accurate analysis of the tension between church tradition and life in the spirit. Those who find themselves in either camp need to realize they not only have gifts for one another, but more importantly, that they

---

5. Kelly D. Silvers "Montanism and the Charismatic Movement in the Spirit-Structure Tension in the History of the Church" (master's thesis, Library at United Theological Seminary, Dayton, Ohio, 1973), pp. 59-60.

need each other if they are to be faithful witnesses to all the biblical truths.

One of the exciting aspects of the charismatic movement is that it spans denominational lines, allowing Christians of different traditions to join together in a variety of common experiences (such as praise and prayer, spiritual healing, worship, Bible study, and fellowship). Equally encouraging are several main-line denominational groups of charismatic-oriented church members who are working actively to maintain the unity of the Spirit within denominational structures. Examples of these groups are found in churches such as the Lutheran, Roman Catholic, Presbyterian, Episcopal, and United Methodist churches.[6]

May all who are baptized into the Christian family be receptive, in an intentional way, to the gifting activity of the Holy Spirit in their lives.

May all perceived gifts of the Holy Spirit be employed by the receivers for the work of ministry, for building up the Body of Christ.

May all who name the name of Jesus Christ as their Lord and Savior be motivated and empowered by the best and the most productive charisma of all, the gift of love.

---

6. United Methodist readers who want to keep current on the charismatic movement in their denomination will want to subscribe to MANNA, a periodical of the United Methodist Renewal Services Fellowship (UMRSF), published at least six times annually for all persons interested in and committed to the renewal movement within The United Methodist Church. Address inquiries to UMRSF, Box 50086, Nashville, Tennessee 37205.

A very helpful statement adopted by the General Conference of The United Methodist Church in 1976 is available from Discipleship Resources, P. O. Box 840, Nashville, Tennessee 37205, titled: "Guidelines: The United Methodist Church and the Charismatic Movement."

GROUP STUDY GUIDE: CHAPTER 7

Materials needed for this session:
A Bible for each participant
Notepaper and pencils
1. THE HOLY SPIRIT AMONG US
   a. The Gifts
      1. Read Acts 2:38, 1 Cor. 12:4-11, Rom. 12:6-8, 1 Cor. 12:28, Eph. 4:11.
      2. Has anyone in the group received any of the Holy Spirit's gifts? (Share and discuss.)
      3. Does anyone know another Christian who has any of the charismata?
   b. The Fruit
      1. Read Romans 12:9-18 and Galatians 5:22-23. Is there evidence of the fruits of the Spirit in the lives of persons in our church?
      2. What are some ways people can be more open and receptive to the Holy Spirit? (List the findings on the board.)
2. LOVE . . . GIFT OR FRUIT OR BOTH?
   Group Exercises
   a. The apostle Paul named love as a fruit of the Spirit (Gal. 5:22), and mentions it in the context of gifts (1 Cor. 12:31 — 14:1). Read these passages and discuss in the group insights and confirmations.
   b. Discuss this statement from p. 94: "A self-righteous or spiritually superior attitude on the part of any Christian (charismatic or non-charismatic) reveals that the Holy Spirit has yet to do his primary work in that Christian: namely, to direct him or her in the more excellent way — the way of love."
3. BLESSED TO BE A BLESSING
   Are we at the end or . . . *the beginning?*
   These are the questions: Are we ending the study on the healing ministry of our church? Or, are we open

to advocating the beginning of an intentional healing
ministry?
*We have been blessed and we are called to be a bless-
ing.*
Here are some considerations:

    Is there a strong consensus within our group to
    advocate an experimental period of healing ser-
    vices in the church?
    What is our plan for working through the chan-
    nels which our church provides? (Make notes on
    paper provided.)
    • Our pastor
    • Our church ministry/administrative board
    • Which liturgy service(s) will we select (see
    Appendix A)?
    • Educational/PR needs within our church
    • Suggested time frame
    • A suitable evaluation instrument
    Note: The two most important beginning consid-
    erations are:
        our group's consensus
        our pastor's openness.

4. THE HOLY SPIRIT GUIDES US
Conclude your time together with a prayer of
thanksgiving for new insights learned and shared,
followed by a time of silent prayer as each group
member becomes receptive to the Holy Spirit's guidance.

APPENDIX A
Nine Liturgies for Public Healing Services

1. A SERVICE OF HEALING*

Before the service: May we prepare ourselves in silence.

"Thou dost keep him in perfect peace whose mind is stayed on thee."

I. Words of Preparation:
   "Come to me, all who labor and are heavy laden, and I will give you rest."
   "For where two or three are gathered in my name, there am I in the midst of them."
   "My peace I give to you."
   "Ask, and it will be given you; seek, and you will find; knock, and it will be opened to you."
   "If you ask anything in my name, I will do it."
II. A Prayer of Invocation (Minister and People)
   ALMIGHTY GOD, UNTO WHOM ALL HEARTS ARE OPEN, ALL DESIRES KNOWN, AND FROM WHOM NO SECRETS ARE HID, CLEANSE THE THOUGHTS OF OUR HEARTS BY THE INSPIRATION OF THY HOLY SPIRIT, THAT WE MAY PERFECTLY LOVE THEE AND WORTHILY MAGNIFY THY HOLY NAME; THROUGH JESUS CHRIST OUR

*Lawrence W. Althouse, *Rediscovering the Gift of Healing* (Nashville: Abingdon, 1977), pp. 139-140.

99

LORD, WHO HATH TAUGHT US WHEN WE PRAY,
"OUR FATHER . . . ."

III. **The Act of Confession**

"While I refused to speak, my body wasted away with moaning all day long. For day and night thy hand was heavy upon me, the sap in me dried up as in a summer drought.

Then I declared my sin, I did not conceal my guilt.

I said, 'With sorrow I will confess my disobedience to the Lord'; then thou didst remit the penalty of my sin." (Psalm 32:3-5 NEB)

A Prayer of General Confession (Minister and people):

ALMIGHTY AND MOST MERCIFUL FATHER; WE HAVE ERRED AND STRAYED FROM THY WAYS LIKE LOST SHEEP. WE HAVE FOLLOWED TOO MUCH THE DEVICES AND DESIRES OF OUR OWN HEARTS. WE HAVE OFFENDED AGAINST THY HOLY LAWS. WE HAVE LEFT UNDONE THINGS WHICH WE OUGHT TO HAVE DONE; AND WE HAVE DONE THOSE THINGS WHICH WE OUGHT NOT TO HAVE DONE; AND THERE IS NO HEALTH IN US. BUT THOU, O LORD, HAVE MERCY UPON US MISERABLE OFFENDERS. SPARE THOU US, O GOD, WHO CONFESS OUR FAULTS. RESTORE THOU THOSE WHO ARE PENITENT; ACCORDING TO THY PROMISES DECLARED UNTO US IN CHRIST JESUS OUR LORD. AND GRANT, O MOST MERCIFUL FATHER, FOR HIS SAKE, THAT WE MAY HEREAFTER LIVE A GODLY, RIGHTEOUS, AND SOBER LIFE, TO THE GLORY OF THY HOLY NAME. AMEN.

The Assurance of Pardon:

If we confess our sins he is faithful and just, and will forgive our sins and cleanse us from all unrighteousness.

IV. **A Hymn of Praise**

V. **A Scripture Reading**   PSALM 51

VI. **A Meditation on the Healing Ministry**

VII. **A Period of Intercession**

"Is any among you suffering? Let him pray.... Is any among you sick? Let him call for the elders of the church, and let them pray over him ... and the prayer of faith will save the sick man, and the Lord will raise him up" (James 5:13-15).

We are met together here as members of Christ's Body, the Church, commissioned to do his healing work on earth. Let us remember that his healing life will flow through us, his channels, to those in need. Let us claim with strong confidence the promise made to all intercessors: ". . . Whatever you ask in prayer, believe that you receive it, and you will."

VIII. **The Ministry of the Laying-on-of-Hands**

Let us now sit back, relaxed and comfortable. Then, with eyes closed, let us gently and trustfully repeat the words of this healing promise:

GOD'S HEALING LOVE IS WITHIN ME.

Let us sit in silence for a few moments until the invitation to come forward is given.

When the invitation is given, you may come forward, one at a time, kneeling at the altar rail to receive the laying-on-of-hands for forgiveness of sin, healing of mind, body, and spirit, personal problems and concerns, either for yourself or others.

Those desiring not to kneel may come forward and sit in the front pew instead.

IX. **A Prayer of Praise and Thanksgiving**

The Doxology (congregation joining)

X. **The Benediction**

"Your faith has made you well; go in peace, and be healed of your disease."

2. A HEALING SERVICE DESIGNED
PRIMARILY TO GLORIFY GOD*

Begin by Praising God
(using psalms, hymns, acts of praise)
Silent Prayer
(We prepare ourselves for God's healing Spirit.)
First, personal meditation on some healing event as revealed in the scriptures. We meditate to the place where we can see Jesus in a particular situation healing the infirm. After we are able to see him clearly in our minds, then we acknowledge his immediate presence among us.
Second, a period of contemplation where, without words, we simply worship him. The 23rd Psalm affirms God without asking for a thing.
Third, we speak to God out of our own personal need, praying only for ourselves.
Fourth, we listen to what God has to say to us.
A Time of Testimony
(We share what God is doing in our lives with regard to his healing ministry.)
Intercessory Concerns and Prayers
(We field requests from persons in the group and someone volunteers to pray specifically for each request.)
Circle of Prayer
(Some persons might request the laying-on-of-hands, at which time several will gather around, again invoking God's healing Spirit.)
Conclusion of the Service
(The minister often annoints each one, using oil and making the sign of the Cross on the forehead, simply praying: "In the name of the Father, the Son, and the Holy Spirit, be healed.")

---

*Robert G. Tuttle, Jr., *The Partakers* (Nashville: Abingdon, 1974), pp. 74-75.

Benediction
(usually sung)

3. A SERVICE OF SACRAMENT AND PRAYER*

The Organ Prelude

A Service of Confession and Sacrament
for the Healing of the Spirit

The Sacrament of Holy Communion

Follow the ritual as found on page 24 in the *Book of Worship*. (The elements will be brought to the worshiper as we kneel in the pew; please retain this until all have been served, and we will partake together at a signal from the minister.)

The Hymn: "What a Friend We Have in Jesus"

A Service of Prayer for the Healing
of the Body

Reading of the Scripture

Hear what our Lord Jesus Christ saith:

Heal the sick . . . and say unto them, The kingdom of God is come nigh unto you. What things soever ye desire when ye pray, believe that ye receive them, and ye shall have them.   — Luke 10:9; Mark 11:24 (KJV)

Hear also what St. James saith:

Is any sick among you? Let him call for the elders of the church; and let them pray over him, anointing him with oil in the name of the Lord: And the prayer of faith shall save the sick, and the Lord shall raise him up; and if he have committed sins, they shall be forgiven him.   — James 5:14-15 (KJV)

Hear also what St. Paul saith:

Be ye transformed by the renewing of your mind. God

---

*Courtesy of the Hyde Park Community United Methodist Church, Dr. Emerson S. Colaw, Senior Minister, located at Observatory and Grace, Cincinnati, Ohio 45208. Local churches may reproduce this liturgy for use by the congregation without seeking permission from The Upper Room.

hath not given us the spirit of fear; but of power, and of love, and of a sound mind.

                    — Romans 12:2; 2 Timothy 1:7 (KJV)

The Meditation   By the Minister

Intercessions

Seeing that we have a great High Priest who has passed into the heavens, Jesus Christ, the Son of God, let us come boldly unto the throne of grace, that we may have mercy, and find grace to help in time of need.

Minister: O God, make speed to help us.

Answer: O LORD, MAKE HASTE TO HELP US.

Minister: The Lord be with you.

Answer: AND WITH THY SPIRIT.

Minister: Let us pray.

Minister: As our Lord has taught us, we have confidence to say OUR FATHER. . . .

Minister: Remembering that all of God's children are near and dear to him, wherever they may be, let us first pray for those who desire our prayers, many of whom cannot be with us this day. Let us pray for those who are ill in body, distressed in mind, or troubled in spirit.

Minister: Blessed Jesus, we bring unto thy loving care and protection, on the stretchers of our prayers, all those who are sick in mind or body or soul. Take from them all fears and help them ever to put their trust in thee, that they may feel beneath them thy everlasting arms. Cleanse them of all resentments, jealousy, self-pity, pride, or anything else that might block thy healing power. Fill them with the sense of thy loving presence, that they may experience the kingdom of love in their hearts. Touch them with thy divine transforming power, that they may be healed and live to glorify thee, to be used by thee to build thy kingdom on earth as it is in heaven. We thank thee. Amen.

Let us now pray for ourselves, first putting ourselves, body, mind, and spirit in the healing presence of Christ.

Moment of Silent Prayer

Minister: Lord, hear our prayer.

Answer: AND LET OUR CRY COME UNTO THEE.

The Affirmation

Minister: O Lord, save thy servants.

Answer: WHO PUT THEIR TRUST IN THEE.

Minister: Send unto them help from above.

Answer: AND EVERMORE MIGHTILY DEFEND THEM.

Minister: As I abide in Christ, I am supplied with all the spiritual resources required for my needs.

Answer: AS I ABIDE IN CHRIST, I AM FREE FROM FEAR AND HAVE QUIETNESS AND CONFIDENCE WITHIN.

Minister: As I abide in Christ, I am at one with God and know the peace of God which passes understanding.

Answer: I CAN DO ALL THINGS THROUGH CHRIST WHO STRENGTHENS ME.

Minister: I believe in the Son of God; therefore I am in him.

Answer: GIVE PEACE FOR ALL TIME, O LORD, AND FILL THE HEARTS OF ALL MEN EVERYWHERE WITH THE SPIRIT OF OUR LORD JESUS CHRIST.

Minister: Who shall separate us from the love of Christ? Shall tribulations or distress, or persecution, or famine, or nakedness or peril or sword?

Minister and People: NAY, IN ALL OF THESE THINGS WE ARE MORE THAN CONQUERORS THROUGH HIM THAT LOVED US.

FOR I AM PERSUADED THAT NEITHER
DEATH, NOR LIFE, NOR ANGELS, NOR
PRINCIPALITIES, NOR POWERS, NOR
THINGS PRESENT, NOR THINGS TO
COME, NOR HEIGHT, NOR DEPTH, NOR
ANY OTHER CREATURE SHALL BE ABLE
TO SEPARATE US FROM THE LOVE OF
GOD, WHICH IS IN CHRIST JESUS OUR
LORD. AMEN.

The Laying-on-of-Hands

The Prayer: The Almighty Lord, who is a most strong
tower to all those who put their trust in him, to whom
all things in heaven, in earth, and under the earth do
bow and obey, be now and evermore your defense;
and make you know and feel that there is none other
name under heaven given to man, in whom, and
through whom you may receive health and salvation,
but only the name of our Lord Jesus Christ. Amen.

(Let each person desiring prayer place on the card the
nature of the request, whether it be for the self or for
another person, and then come forward, hand this to
the minister, and kneel.)

Thanksgiving

Minister: Lift up your hearts.

Answer: WE LIFT THEM UP UNTO THE LORD.

Minister: Let us give thanks unto our Lord God.

Answer: IT IS MEET AND RIGHT SO TO DO.

Minister: It is very meet, right, and our bounden
duty, that we should at all times, and in all
places, give thanks unto thee O Lord, Holy
Father, the giver of health and salvation;
whose only-begotten Son came into the
world that we might have life, and have it
abundantly; who in his love for persons
ministered to their bodily infirmities, and
gave both power and commandment to his
disciples likewise to heal the sick; we yield
thee hearty thanks and most high praise
that thou hast this day continued thy heal-

ing work among us. Make us ever mindful of thy mercies, that we may continue thy faithful servants unto our life's end; through Jesus Christ our Lord. Amen.

The Benediction

God the Father, God the Son, God the Holy Spirit, bless, preserve, and keep you; the Lord mercifully with his favor look upon you, and fill you with all spiritual benediction and grace, that ye may so live in this life, that in the world to come ye may have life everlasting. Amen.

4. A LITURGY FOR THE SERVICE OF HEALING AND HOLY COMMUNION*

"As the mountains are round about Jerusalem, so the Lord is round about his people, from this time forth and for evermore."   —Psalm 125:2

Organ Prelude

Greetings and Introductions

Hymn

Responsive Reading

Leader: I lift up my eyes to the hills. From whence does my help come?

People: MY HELP COMES FROM THE LORD, WHO MADE HEAVEN AND EARTH.

Leader: He will not let your foot to be moved, he who keeps you will not slumber.

People: BEHOLD, HE WHO KEEPS ISRAEL WILL NEITHER SLUMBER NOR SLEEP.

---

*Courtesy of the Columbia Heights United Methodist Church, William C. Miller (Pastor), address: 91 Sturbridge Road, Columbus, Ohio 43228. Liturgy designed by Ruth Strickland, March 1979. Local churches may reproduce this liturgy for use by the congregation without seeking permission from The Upper Room.

Leader: The Lord is your keeper. The Lord is your
          shade on your right hand.
People: THE SUN WILL NOT SMITE THEE BY DAY,
          NOR THE MOON BY NIGHT.
Leader: The Lord will keep you from all evil; he will
          keep your life.
People: THE LORD WILL KEEP YOUR GOING OUT
          AND YOUR COMING IN FROM THIS TIME
          FORTH AND FOR EVERMORE. AMEN.
          (Psalm 121:8)

Hymn

A Good Word for Today

Moments of Personal Reflection and Meditation

Call to Confession and Forgiveness

Leader: Let us examine our lives, and let us confess
          our sins to God, our merciful Father.
Unison: ALMIGHTY AND MOST MERCIFUL GOD,
          WHO KNOWS THE THOUGHTS OF OUR
          HEARTS, WE CONFESS THAT WE HAVE
          SINNED AGAINST YOU. WE HAVE TRANS-
          GRESSED YOUR HOLY LAWS. WE HAVE
          NEGLECTED YOUR WORD. FORGIVE US, O
          LORD, WE BESEECH YOU; AND GIVE US
          GRACE AND POWER TO PUT AWAY ALL
          HURTFUL THINGS, THAT, BEING DE-
          LIVERED FROM THE BONDAGE OF SIN,
          WE MAY BRING FORTH FRUIT WORTHY OF
          REPENTANCE, AND HENCEFORTH MAY
          EVER WALK IN YOUR HOLY WAYS,
          THROUGH JESUS CHRIST OUR LORD.
          AMEN.

Assurance of Pardon

Leader: Jesus teaches us, "Whatever you ask in
          prayer, believe that you receive it, and you
          will. And whenever you stand praying, for-
          give, if you have anything against any one;
          so that your father who is in heaven may
          forgive you your trespasses."
                                        — Mark 11:24-25

Hymn Prayers of Intercession
Reading of names of prayer request.

Leader: Let us pray.

Unison: O LORD IT IS SO GOOD TO THINK YOU ARE
THE ONE WHO KEEPS THE STARS ON
THEIR COURSE, THE ONE WHO CREATED
THE EXPANSE WE CALL UNIVERSE. THAT
IS A VERY COMFORTABLE, REASSURING
THOUGHT. BUT LORD, WE KNOW THAT IN
ADDITION TO GUIDING THE UNIVERSE,
YOU WANT US TO CARE ABOUT EACH
OTHER. AND YOU WANT US TO FORGIVE,
AND THAT IS VERY DIFFICULT AND
SOMETIMES IMPOSSIBLE TO DO ALONE.
THEREFORE, WE PRAY THAT YOU WILL
COME CLOSER TO EACH OF THESE PER-
SONS, THAT THEY WILL KNOW YOU ARE
NEAR THEM. HELP US ALL TO KNOW
THAT STILL SMALL VOICE WITHIN. HELP
US TO LOOK UP TO THE HILLS YOU HAVE
MADE, AND MAY WE BE POINTED
BEYOND TO YOUR GRACE, YOUR LOVE, TO
YOUR HEALING POWER, AND DIVINE
GUIDANCE. WE ASK ALL THESE THINGS
IN THE NAME OF OUR LORD AND SAVIOR.
AMEN.

Commissioning of the Prayer Team by the Pastor
Healing Through the Holy Communion
Prayers for Personal Healings
You may come forward for healing prayers and laying-
on-of-hands for yourself, your family, or friends, or
you may remain seated, keeping your focus on the
Christ who heals the body, mind, spirit, and relation-
ships.

A Time of Sharing Our Thanksgivings
Hymn "Praise the Lord"   (tune: "Edelweiss")
Benediction
Go in peace and the peace of Christ go with you.
Amen.

5. ORDER OF SERVICE FOR PRAYER, MEDITATION, AND SPIRITUAL HEALING*

The Period of Quiet Meditation
During the playing of the familiar hymns may our thoughts turn to the love of God and may our prayer be:
"Breathe on me, Breath of God,
Till I am wholly Thine,
Until this earthly part of me
Glows with Thy fire divine."
The Praise
The Call to Worship   Minister
Draw nigh to God, and he will draw nigh to you. Enter into his gates with thanksgiving, and into his courts with praise. All things whatsoever ye shall ask in prayer, believing, ye shall receive. Glory ye in God's holy name: seek the Lord and his strength: let the heart of them rejoice that seek the Lord.
The Invocation   Minister and People
O THOU, IN WHOSE LIFE WE FIND OUR LIFE, THROUGH THE GIFT OF WHOSE SPIRIT WE DO OUR WORK AND BEAR OUR BURDENS; GRANT US NOW THE SENSE OF THY NEARNESS. WE WOULD OPEN OUR HEARTS FREELY TO THY SPIRIT, OUR MINDS TO THY LAW, AND OUR WILLS TO THY QUICKENING ENERGY. DWELL IN US AND MAKE US FRUITFUL. WE ASK IN CHRIST'S NAME. AMEN.
The Responsive Reading
The Prayer of Thanksgiving   Minister and People
O LORD OUR GOD, THE AUTHOR AND GIVER OF ALL GOOD THINGS, WE THANK THEE FOR ALL THY MERCIES, AND FOR THY LOVING CARE OVER ALL THY CREATURES. WE BLESS THEE FOR THE GIFT OF LIFE; FOR THY PROTECTION ROUND ABOUT US; FOR THY GUIDING HAND UPON US; AND FOR ALL

---

*Courtesy of Central College United Presbyterian Church, Richard D. Ellsworth, Senior Minister, address: 6891 Sunbury Road, Westerville, Ohio 43081. Local churches may reproduce this liturgy for use by the congregation without seeking permission from The Upper Room.

THE TOKENS OF THY LOVE. WE THANK THEE FOR FRIENDSHIP AND DUTY; FOR GOOD HOPES AND PRECIOUS MEMORIES; FOR THE JOYS THAT CHEER US; AND THE TRIALS THAT TEACH US TO TRUST IN THEE. MOST OF ALL WE THANK THEE FOR THE SAVING KNOWLEDGE OF THY SON OUR SAVIOR; FOR THE LIVING PRESENCE OF THY SPIRIT, THE COMFORTER; FOR THY CHURCH, THE BODY OF CHRIST; FOR THE MINISTRY OF WORD AND SACRAMENT; FOR ALL THE MEANS OF GRACE; AND FOR THE HOPE OF GLORY.

IN ALL THESE THINGS, O HEAVENLY FATHER, MAKE US WISE UNTO A RIGHT USE OF THY BENEFITS; THAT WE MAY RENDER AN ACCEPTABLE THANKSGIVING UNTO THEE ALL THE DAYS OF OUR LIFE. THROUGH JESUS CHRIST OUR LORD. AMEN.

God's Word to Us

The Reading of the Scriptures

The Meditation on God's Word

Our Confession

The Prayer of Confession   Minister and People

MOST HOLY AND MERCIFUL FATHER; WE ACKNOWLEDGE AND CONFESS BEFORE THEE; OUR SINFUL NATURE PRONE TO EVIL AND SLOTHFUL IN GOOD; AND ALL OUR SHORTCOMINGS AND OFFENSES. THOU ALONE KNOWEST HOW OFTEN WE HAVE SINNED; IN WANDERING FROM THY WAYS; IN WASTING THY GIFTS; IN FORGETTING THY LOVE. BUT THOU, O LORD, HAVE MERCY UPON US; WHO ARE ASHAMED AND SORRY FOR ALL WHEREIN WE HAVE DISPLEASED THEE. TEACH US TO HATE OUR ERRORS; CLEANSE US FROM OUR SECRET FAULTS; AND FORGIVE OUR SINS; FOR THE SAKE OF THY DEAR SON. AND O MOST HOLY AND LOVING FATHER; HELP US, WE BESEECH THEE; TO LIVE IN THY LIGHT AND WALK IN THY WAYS; ACCORDING TO THE COMMANDMENTS OF JESUS CHRIST OUR LORD. AMEN.

Confession in Silent Prayer

The Assurance of Pardon   Minister

Almighty God, who doth freely pardon all who repent

and turn to him, now fulfill in every contrite heart the promise of redeeming grace; remitting all our sins, and cleansing us from all evil conscience; through the perfect sacrifice of Christ Jesus our Lord. Amen.

The Intercession

Prayer of Preparation   In Unison

O GOD, THE SOVEREIGN GOOD OF THE SOUL, WHO REQUIREST THE HEARTS OF ALL THY CHILDREN, DELIVER US FROM ALL SLOTH IN THY WORK, ALL COLDNESS IN THY CAUSE; AND GRANT US BY LOOKING UNTO THEE TO REKINDLE OUR LOVE, AND BY WAITING UPON THEE TO RENEW OUR STRENGTH.

HEAR US NOW, WE BESEECH THEE, AS WE WOULD BRING TO THEE OUR PRAYERS OF LOVE AND CONCERN FOR THESE WHOM WE NAME BEFORE THEE. ENFOLD THEM WITH THY PERFECT LOVE AND BRING TO EACH THE TOUCH OF HEALING WHICH WE KNOW IS THY WILL. FOR THIS WE ASK IN THE NAME AND SPIRIT OF CHRIST JESUS, OUR LORD. AMEN.

The Silent Moment of Intercession

After the giving of the requests let each of us hold the persons for whom we are praying up into the light of God's holy presence. In our imagination may we see these people not as ones who are sick, but as persons being made whole in body, mind, and soul by the healing touch of the master Physician.

The Moment of Submission

The General Prayer   In Unison

ALMIGHTY AND IMMORTAL GOD, GIVER OF LIFE AND HEALTH, GRANT TO US NOW THE WONDERFUL TOUCH OF THY HEALING LOVE. FLOOD OUR LIVES WITH THE LIGHT AND WARMTH OF THY PRESENCE. BRING RELEASE FROM ALL WEARINESS, BITTERNESS, AND ANXIETY. AS IN TRUE HUMILITY WE KNEEL BEFORE THEE, MAY WE RECEIVE THE TOUCH OF HEALING WHICH COMES THROUGH THIS ONE WHO IS THE MASTER PHYSICIAN. AMEN.

**The Moment of Individual Dedication and
the Laying-on-of-Hands**
Each person is invited to come to the chancel step to
receive the laying-on-of-hands with prayer. Come in
simple faith, looking up to Jesus who is the master
Physician. Or if you choose to remain seated, remember that the healing, forgiving touch of the Master is
yours but for the asking.
The Pronouncement of Healing   Minister
and the Benediction

6. SERVICE OF SPIRITUAL HEALING

Organ Meditation
Call to Worship   The Minister
*Hymn
Prayer for the Presence of Christ   In Unison
O LIVING CHRIST, DRAW NEAR TO US NOW, AS WE
DRAW NEAR TO YOU, AND IN THIS QUIET AND
SACRED HOUR, BE THE HOPE AND PEACE OF OUR
SOULS. MAKE US CONSCIOUS OF YOUR HEALING
NEARNESS. TOUCH OUR EYES THAT WE MAY SEE
YOU. OPEN OUR EARS THAT WE MAY HEAR YOUR
VOICE. ENTER OUR HEARTS THAT WE MAY KNOW
YOUR LOVE. OVERSHADOW OUR SOULS AND
BODIES WITH YOUR PRESENCE, YOUR LOVE, AND
YOUR HEALING LIFE. IN YOUR NAME WE PRAY.
AMEN.
Call to Confession   The Minister
Prayer of Confession   Minister and People
MOST MERCIFUL GOD, WE CONFESS THAT WE
HAVE SINNED AGAINST YOU IN THOUGHT, WORD,
AND DEED; WE HAVE NOT LOVED YOU WITH OUR
WHOLE HEART, NOR HAVE WE LOVED OUR NEIGH-
BORS AS OURSELVES. FORGIVE WHAT WE HAVE

*Courtesy of the Westwood United Methodist Church, Cincinnati,
Ohio, 45211, Dr. Paul Vandegriff, Senior Minister. Local churches
may reproduce this liturgy for use by the congregation without seeking permission from The Upper Room.

114 *Blessed to Be a Blessing*

BEEN; HELP US TO AMEND WHAT WE ARE, AND
WITH THE HELP OF YOUR SPIRIT DIRECT WHAT WE
SHALL BE; THAT WE MAY DELIGHT IN YOUR WILL
AND WALK IN YOUR WAYS; THROUGH JESUS
CHRIST OUR LORD. AMEN.

Words of Assurance   The Minister

*Gloria Patri

*The Passing of the Peace

Minister: The peace of the Lord be with you.

People: AND WITH YOU ALSO.

Minister and People turn to one another throughout
the congregation: THE PEACE OF THE LORD BE
WITH YOU.

Scripture Reading

Message

Prayers of Intercession

Litany of Intercession

Leader: We beseech you to hear us, O Lord, that you
will grant your healing grace to all who are
physically sick, injured or disabled, that
they may be made whole.

People: LORD, HEAR OUR PRAYER.

Leader: That you will mend all broken relationships,
and restore all who are in mental turmoil or
emotional distress, to soundness of mind
and cheerfulness of spirit.

People: LORD, HEAR OUR PRAYER.

Leader: That you will bless physicians, nurses, and
all who minister to the suffering: granting
them wisdom and faith, skill and sympathy,
tenderness and patience.

People: LORD, HEAR OUR PRAYER.

Leader: That you will restore to wholeness, brokenness of any kind, in our nation and in the
world.

People: LORD, HEAR OUR PRAYER.

Leader: We pray in the name of Christ who taught

us to pray together: "Our Father who art in heaven, hallowed be thy name. . . ."

The Laying-on-of-Hands and Anointing with Oil

Minister: Seeing that we have a great High Priest who has passed into the heavens, Jesus Christ, the Son of God, let us come boldly to the throne of grace.

(Here people desiring the laying-on-of-hands and anointing with oil may come forward.)

Prayer of Thanksgiving	The Minister
Benediction	The Minister
Postlude	

7. A WORSHIP EXPERIENCE
OF PRAYER, HEALING, AND HOLY COMMUNION*

Meditation Music
Call to Worship
The Confession

Leader: Let us confess our sin to God, our merciful Father.

All: ALMIGHTY GOD, FATHER OF OUR LORD JESUS CHRIST, MAKER OF ALL THINGS, JUDGE OF ALL PEOPLE, WE ADMIT AND CONFESS OUR SINFULNESS. WE HAVE TURNED AWAY FROM EACH OTHER IN OUR THINKING, SPEAKING, AND DOING. WE HAVE DONE THE EVIL YOU FORBID AND HAVE NOT DONE THE GOOD YOU DEMAND. WE DO REPENT AND ARE TRULY SORRY FOR THESE OUR SINS. HAVE MERCY ON US, KIND FATHER, BECAUSE OF THE OBEDIENCE OF OUR BROTHER, JESUS CHRIST, YOUR SON. FORGIVE US, AND WITH THE POWER OF THE HOLY

---

*Liturgy designed by Nicholas Itzzes and James Wagner, Fall, 1974. Local churches may reproduce this liturgy for use by the congregation without seeking permission from The Upper Room.

SPIRIT MOVE US TO SERVE YOU FAITH-
FULLY. SET OUR FEET UPON THE NEW
PATH OF LIFE, AND BE OUR RULER AND
LORD.

Leader: God has promised forgiveness of sins to
those who repent and turn to him. May he
keep you in his grace by the Holy Spirit,
lead you to greater faith and obedience, and
bring you to live with him forever, through
Jesus Christ, our Lord.

People: AMEN.

The Lessons

The Homily

Silence

(Personal Prayer, Meditation, Confession)
"Commune with your own hearts . . . and be silent."
                                                    —Psalm 4:4
" 'Be still, and know that I am God. I am exalted
among the nations, I am exalted in the earth!' The
Lord of hosts is with us; the God of Jacob is our
refuge."   —Psalm 46:10-11

Corporate Concerns and Prayer Requests

Intercessory Prayer

Holy Communion and Healing Ministry

You are invited to come forward to participate in
the Holy Communion, and to receive the laying-on-of-
hands with prayer and anointing oil (James 5:13-16).
Come in simple, sincere faith, looking up to Christ
Jesus who is the divine Savior and Physician.

Or, if you choose to remain seated, remember that
the healing, forgiving touch of the Master is yours for
the asking.

Prayers of Thanksgiving

Benediction

Meditation Music

8. A WORSHIP SERVICE OF HOLY COMMUNION
AND SPIRITUAL HEALING*

Upon Entering the Chapel

"Our purpose as Christians is not to impress persons with how good we are, but to love them so they will know how good they are."

Fr. John Powell, S. J.

Musical Prelude

A time of personal meditation and prayer.

Words of Welcome and Introduction to the Gathered Community

The Call to Intentional Worship of God in the Name of the Father, the Son, and Holy Spirit. Amen.

Acts of Praise and Adoration of God

This may include hymns, psalms, prayers.

An Affirmation of Faith (unison)

    I BELIEVE IN THE LIVING GOD,
        THE FATHER OF ALL HUMANKIND,
        WHO CREATES AND SUSTAINS THE
        UNIVERSE
        BY HIS POWER AND IN HIS LOVE.
    I BELIEVE IN JESUS CHRIST, HIS SON,
        THE MAN OF NAZARETH;
        BECAUSE OF HIS WORDS AND WORK,
        HIS WAY WITH OTHERS,
        HIS OWN SUFFERING,
        HIS CONQUEST OF DEATH,
        I KNOW WHAT HUMAN LIFE OUGHT TO BE
        AND WHAT GOD IS LIKE.
    I BELIEVE THAT THE SPIRIT OF GOD IS
        PRESENT WITH US, NOW AND ALWAYS,
        AND HIS HEALING CAN BE EXPERIENCED
        IN PRAYER, IN FORGIVENESS,

*Courtesy of the First United Methodist Church, Two South College Street, Athens, Ohio 45701. Ministers: David M. Griebner and James K. Wagner. Local churches may reproduce this liturgy for use by the congregation without seeking permission from The Upper Room.

IN THE WORD, THE SACRAMENTS,
THE FELLOWSHIP OF THE CHURCH
AND IN ALL WE DO. AMEN.

A Reading from the Holy Bible

The Sharing of a Good Word for Today

May be related to the scripture reading, or a personal
testimony, homily, or dialogue.

Moments of Personal Reflection

The Call to Confession and Forgiveness

(Unison)

ALMIGHTY GOD, OUR LOVING FATHER, YOU
CREATED US FOR LIFE TOGETHER. WE CONFESS
THAT WE HAVE TURNED FROM YOUR WILL. WE
HAVE NOT LOVED ONE ANOTHER AS YOU COM-
MANDED.

WE HAVE BEEN QUICK TO CLAIM OUR OWN
RIGHTS AND BE CARELESS OF THE RIGHTS OF
OTHERS. WE HAVE TAKEN MUCH AND GIVEN LIT-
TLE.

FORGIVE OUR DISOBEDIENCE, O GOD, AND
STRENGTHEN US IN LOVE, SO THAT WE MAY SERVE
YOU AS A FAITHFUL PEOPLE, AND LIVE TOGETHER
IN YOUR JOY, THROUGH JESUS CHRIST, OUR LORD
AND SAVIOR. AMEN.

Moments of Personal Confession

Words of Assurance and Pardon

Jesus says to you and to me: "Be of good cheer; your
sins are forgiven. Go and sin no more.

Do not condemn or punish yourself. Our heavenly
Father accepts you as you are, the good and the bad
all wrapped up together. Whatever you have done,
you are free from bondage to your past and from
anxiety for your future.

You are free to live fully in the present. Life is good.
Be not afraid.

This is the day that the Lord has made, rejoice and
be glad in it.

Arise! Pick up your life and walk in my power and
peace and grace."

(Unison)
GLORY BE TO THE FATHER AND TO THE SON AND
TO THE HOLY GHOST. AS IT WAS IN THE BEGINNING
IS NOW AND EVER SHALL BE, WORLD WITHOUT
END. AMEN! AMEN!

Hymn
Prayer of Intercession for Others (responsively)
O Lord, we pray for the family and the home,
> AND FOR THOSE WHO ARE LONELY AND FOR-
> GOTTEN.

We pray for our systems of law and order,
> AND FOR THOSE WHO SUFFER INJUSTICE.

We pray for our varied religious forms,
> AND FOR DIVISIONS CREATED BY NARROW-
> MINDEDNESS.

We pray for our schools and colleges,
> AND FOR THOSE WHO ARE DENIED THESE BENE-
> FITS.

We pray for our complex system of industry and busi-
ness,
> AND FOR THOSE WHO ARE UNABLE TO FIND
> WORK.

We pray for our institutions of international peace and
understanding,
> AND FOR THOSE WHO ARE THIS DAY SUBJECTED
> TO THE PAIN AND DEATH OF WAR.

We pray for our churches and our hospitals,
> AND FOR THOSE WHO ARE SICK OF SPIRIT, MIND,
> AND BODY.

And especially we pray for:
> (Someone will read names on the prayer list.) EACH
> ONE AND EACH SITUATION WE LIFT UP INTO
> YOUR LIGHT AND LOVE, THANKING YOU FOR
> HELPING AND HEALING, AND GIVING YOU THE
> GLORY. AMEN.

Commissioning of the Praying Teams
"In the name of the Lord Jesus Christ, by his author-

ity and power, we do commission you to be an instrument of his healing love. Amen."

The Sacrament of Holy Communion

Prayers for Personal Healings of Body, Mind, Spirit, and Relationships.
Feel free to make any request known to the praying team. Come forward for yourself or on behalf of someone else. Come forward expectantly keeping your mind and heart on the healing Christ. Come forward to receive the anointing oil with prayer and the laying-on-of-hands.

A Time of Sharing our Thanksgivings
Benediction
Go in peace and the peace of Christ go with you.

9. A WORSHIP SERVICE OF HOLY COMMUNION AND SPIRITUAL HEALING*

A Time of Personal Meditation and Prayer
Words of Welcome to the Gathered Christian Community
An Act of Praise "Psalm 103" (responsively)
    Leader: Bless the Lord, O my soul;
                 and all that is within me,
                 bless his holy name!
    People: BLESS THE LORD, O MY SOUL, AND FORGET NOT ALL HIS BENEFITS:
    Leader: Who forgives all your iniquity,
                 who heals all your diseases;
    People: WHO REDEEMS YOUR LIFE FROM THE PIT, WHO CROWNS YOU WITH STEADFAST LOVE AND MERCY. AMEN.

---

*Order of Service designed by James K. Wagner.
Holy Communion Liturgy taken from *Ventures in Worship, No. 2*, ed. D. J. Randolph (Nashville: Abingdon, 1970), p. 133.

Prayer of Confession (unison)
ALMIGHTY GOD, UNTO WHOM ALL HEARTS ARE
OPEN, ALL DESIRES KNOWN, AND FROM WHOM NO
SECRETS ARE HIDDEN; CLEANSE THE THOUGHTS
OF OUR HEARTS BY THE INSPIRATION OF THY
HOLY SPIRIT, THAT WE MAY PERFECTLY LOVE
THEE, AND WORTHILY MAGNIFY THY HOLY NAME;
THROUGH JESUS CHRIST OUR LORD. AMEN.

Moments of Personal Confession (in silence)

Assurance of Pardon

Leader: If we confess our sins, he is faithful and just
to forgive us our sins, and to cleanse us from
all unrighteousness. Amen.

A Reading from Holy Scriptures

Prayers for Others

Leader: It has been said that intercessory prayer is
love on its knees. Let all of us be in an attitude of loving concern as the prayer requests are now read:

Expression of Concerns (Someone reads names aloud.)

Leader: Join me now in this prayer of intercession:

Unison: O GOD, WHO ART THE ONLY SOURCE OF
HEALTH AND HEALING, THE SPIRIT OF
CALM AND THE CENTRAL PEACE OF THIS
UNIVERSE, MAKE THESE FOR WHOM WE
NOW PRAY VERY CONSCIOUS OF THY
HEALING NEARNESS. TOUCH THEIR EYES
THAT THEY MAY SEE THEE; OPEN THEIR
EARS THAT THEY MAY HEAR THY VOICE;
ENTER THEIR HEARTS THAT THEY MAY
KNOW THY LOVE. OVERSHADOW THEIR
SOULS AND BODIES WITH THY PRES-
ENCE, THAT THEY MAY PARTAKE OF THY
STRENGTH, THY LOVE, THY LIFE ABUN-
DANT. IN JESUS' NAME WE PRAY. AMEN.

The Sacrament of Holy Communion

Prayer of Consecration (by the Minister)

O God of might and fatherly love, who sent Jesus
to die in order that we might find real life; and who
in that one act of self-giving set everything right

Blessed to Be a Blessing

that humankind made wrong; and who has asked us
to enter into that act by re-enacting it:
O God, help each of us to become more Christlike
as we receive this bread and this wine. May these
elements involve us in Jesus' life, death, and resurrection.
For it was on the very night that he was betrayed
that he took bread, prayed over it, broke it, gave it
to his followers, and said to them, "This is my body
which is broken for you; eat this as a memorial of
me." In the same way after a prayer of thanks he
gave them the wine cup and said to them, "This cup
is God's new covenant sealed by my blood. Whenever you take refreshment do it in memory of me."
Amen.
Prayer of the People
It is not our goodness but yours that brings us to
the table, O God. By ourselves we deserve crumbs,
but you give us a banquet. Bring us such renewal in
this Sacrament, O God, that life will take on new
meaning, we may become more like Christ, and as
we are embraced by his love, let that love shine
through us. Amen.
The Invitation (by the Minister)
The table of the Lord is open to all who accept
Jesus Christ as Lord and Savior and who know they
are in need of his saving grace.
Prayers for Personal Healings
Those who have personal prayer requests may
remain kneeling at the communion railing; the
others may return to their seats. Anointing with oil
and laying-on-of-hands with prayer are offered to
those who request this sacramental ministry.
A Time of Sharing Our Thanksgivings
Benediction
Leader: Go in peace!
People: AND THE PEACE OF CHRIST GO WITH YOU!

APPENDIX B
Resources for Healing Prayer and Meditation

1. THE UPPER ROOM PRAYER MINISTRY

NASHVILLE, TENNESSEE

If you have a need for prayer, call
The Upper Room Living Prayer Center
Toll-Free 1-800-251-2468
(In Tennessee Call Collect 0-615-327-HOPE)

Someone will pray with you and share your request with Upper Room Covenant Groups across the nation. These are intercessory prayer groups composed of concerned, caring Christians.

You may also be interested in having one of the Upper Room trained resource persons come to your church to conduct a Weekend Adventure of Living Prayer. This school of prayer teaches the basic ingredients essential for developing a life of prayer. Persons are inspired and motivated to become intentional in their prayer pilgrimage.

To learn more about the Upper Room Prayer Center, the opportunity to organize a Covenant Prayer Group in your church, and the Weekend Adventure of Living Prayer, contact:

> *Danny E. Morris, Director*
> *Developing Ministries*
> *The Upper Room*
> *1908 Grand Avenue*
> *Nashville, Tennessee 37202*

2. A SPIRITUAL DAILY DOZEN*

by Dr. Alfred W. Price

Consists of twelve "setting up" exercises to be repeated first thing each morning while you breathe deeply of the "Breath of Life." These sayings emphasize the Presence of God and help you prepare for meditation. You might like to do these exercises sitting on the edge of your bed in the quiet of your room or as soon as you arrive at your favorite devotional nook.

1. You are God, in whom I have placed all my trust.
2. Your Presence is everywhere.
3. Your Presence surrounds me; in you I live and move and have my being.
4. Your Presence is within me, strengthening me, inspiring, healing, and perfecting me.
5. Your Presence erases fear, worry, and anxiety.
6. Your Presence gives me strength for all my needs.
7. Your Presence gives me confidence and courage in every situation.
8. Your Presence drives out resentment and hatred, and subdues anger.
9. The inspiration of your Presence gives me understanding, that I may have clearness of vision, steadfastness of thought, and trueness of speech.
10. Your Presence enables me to cope with evil and with disease.
11. Nothing can separate me from your Presence.
12. Praise be to you, O Lord, who gives me victory, through Jesus Christ, my Savior.

In order to keep your mind on God's Presence throughout the day, you may want to write down these sayings and carry them with you for quick reference or post them on a refrigerator door or bathroom mirror.

---

*Doris Moffat, *Christian Meditation* (Chappaqua, New York: Christian Herald Books, 1979), pp. 20-21.

3. HOW TO PRAY FOR ONE'S OWN HEALING*

by the Reverend John H. Parke,
Past Warden of the Order of St. Luke the Physician

1. **Realize**
   Know that you were born for a glorious, triumphant, and whole life, that the will of God for you is good, that the Great Physician wills wholeness for you.
2. **Repent**
   Not all illness is caused by sin, but usually somewhere, somehow, a physical or moral law of the universe has been broken, willfully or accidentally, either by you or by someone closely affecting your life. Insofar as you may have been at fault, confession and a sincere desire to change is needed. Where another may be responsible, your forgiveness of that person is required (Mark 11:25-26; James 5:16). Put away all hostility toward conditions, circumstances, persons, places, and things.
3. **Relax**
   Consciously release all the tensons of your body, all the doubts and anxieties of your mind. Lay aside all criticism, prejudices, and preconceived notions, and keep an open mind. Let go and let God.
4. **Visualize Perfect Health**
   Reverse the negative patterns of disease, limitation, and troubles. Do not syndicate your ills and complaints. Using your imagination, see yourself the way you believe God wants you to be—perfect wholeness in every part of your being—body, mind and spirit. Visualize Jesus, the Great Physician, reaching forward to touch you. As you feel His

---

*John H. Parke, "How to Pray for Healing," *Sharing* Magazine, July, 1973, pp. 16-17. The International Order of St. Luke the Physician, 1212 Wilmer Avenue, Richmond, Virginia 23227. By permission.

touch, know that His healing power is flowing within you.

5. **Ask**

   And you shall receive (Matthew 7:7). "Whatsoever ye shall ask in my name, that will I do" (John 14:13). Ask with faith — "Lord, I believe" (Mark 9:24). "Believe that you have received it, and it will be yours" (Mark 11:24). Ask with thanksgiving — "Father, I thank thee that thou hast heard me" (John 11:41). Even before any results are evident, start thanking God that his healing power is at work. Ask with joy — "Jesus, I praise you. Jesus, I love you" — just pour out your heart in praise and love to him.

6. **Accept**

   Let God touch every area of your life with his power. Realize God's presence continually. Live in the now, think in the now, and act in the now. Live in a constant state of expectancy of God's constant adequacy.

7. **Do Something in Response to Your Healing**

   Do something that you could not do before. Do something for someone else who needs you. Do something special for God. Witness to all what God has done for you.

4. STEPS FOR HEALING PRAYER— A PERSONAL MEDITATION

by Sister Joyce Pranger

1. Quiet place free from noise and distractions.
2. Have a set time.
3. Take a comfortable position, yet disciplined enough to prevent sleep or undue distractions.
4. Localize yourself in the Presence of the Trinity.
5. Consciously start from the head and go through all the parts of the body commanding each part to give up any tension and replace it with complete relaxation. Enjoy the fruit of feeling whole physically.

6. Descend into the deeper layers of your unconscious where you will meet God—without words, without images. Deep faith is important—that Jesus is healing.

7. Removing the "stone" in our lives, any injury, injustice, unforgiveness, greed, selfishness, pride, ambition, etc. Learn to let go in a spirit of childlike faith.

8. Feel a oneness with that person who has caused us suffering.

9. Visualize Jesus touching that area that needs healing.

10. Picture yourself as being totally healed. Agnes Sanford calls this process of picturing oneself already healed a "visualization."

11. All true healing begins in prayer, whether it be a physical healing, psychic healing, or a spiritual healing.

12. A spirit of gratitude of knowing that God has heard our prayer and we are healed. We act on the conviction that God has already heard our prayer and is progressively healing us, even when there is not an instant manifestation.

To learn more about contemplative prayer, contact Sister Joyce in care of The Hermitage, 810 Crosslanes Drive #23, Nitro, West Virginia 25143.

5. A PRIVATE DEVOTIONAL EXERCISE ON FORGIVENESS

by Mary Lou Wagner

In the quiet of your room or your favorite devotional spot, take some unhurried time to ponder these thoughts:

When someone hurts me or fails to meet my expectations, am I able to forgive them immediately without harboring a grudge and without frequently rehearsing my grievance in my mind?

If the answer is no, what are some of the ways my resentment works itself out in my life and in my attitude toward that person?

How do I feel about that person?

How do I feel about myself?

(Do not rush.)

Next, make a list of persons you cannot stand to be around,

who have been unkind to you,
who go out of their way to hurt you,
who insist on their own way,
who do not listen to you,
who constantly try to change you,
who put you down.

Then check out how you feel about yourself.

Do you need to forgive yourself?

What about your relationship with God?

Are you upset or angry with God?

Do you feel he has let you down?

Ask God, in your own sincere way, to forgive you and to cleanse you of all resentment and hurt feelings. As the love begins to flow from God to you and from you to God, ask God to fill you with his peace and joy.

Now, return to your list of persons, lifting up each one by name into the light and love of the healing, forgiving Christ. Intentionally forgive each one, just as God through Christ forgives you.

(Take your time.)

Offer your personal prayer of thanksgiving.

Amen.

APPENDIX C
Cassette Tapes
on the Healing Ministry

1. By Lawrence Althouse
   "Healing & Miracles in the Historic Church"
   "A Service of Healing"
   "A Healing Meditation"
   Available from:
   STAR, 632 S. Locust Street
   Elizabethtown, PA 17022
2. By Don Bartow
   "The Ministry of Healing" (Six 90-minute tapes)
   "A Spiritual Healing Seminar" (Nine lectures)
   "The Inner Healing Messages" (Two 90-minute tapes)
   "The Ecumenical Conference" (Nine 90-minute tapes)
   "The Gifts of the Spirit" (Six 90-minute tapes)
   "Dare to Be a Spiritual Leader" (Set of 12 tapes)
   Available from:
   LIFE ENRICHMENT PUBLISHERS
   Box 526, Canton, OH 44701
3. CHARIS BOOKS & TAPES
   P. O. Box 1232, Jonesboro, AR 72401
   Catalog of listening material will be sent upon request.
4. Order of St. Luke Tape Library. Current catalog will be sent upon request.
   ST. LUKE'S PRESS
   61 Broad Street, Elizabeth, NJ 02701

5. By David Seamands, "The Biblical Psychology Series"
   Tape Ministries
   Box 3389, Pasadena, CA 91103
6. Cassette Tapes from:
   Laity Lodge
   P. O. Box 670, Kerrville, TX 78028
7. Numerous Tapes on Healing from:
   Brother Mandus
   World Healing Crusade
   Blackpool, FY4 1JF
   ENGLAND
8. Dr. O. Carl Simonton of Oncology Associates, Fort Worth, Texas (a medical doctor and cancer expert) has had remarkable success in treating cancer patients with a combination of chemotherapy, psychotherapy, and meditation. This approach is explained in a set of cassette tapes and brochure available from:
   Cognetics, Inc.
   P. O. Box 592
   Saratoga, CA 95070

APPENDIX D
Teaching Conferences
on the Healing Ministry

1. Pastor Don Bartow
   Westminster United Presbyterian Church
   171 Aultman Avenue N.W., Canton, OH 44708
   Mid-week conferences are held twice each year,
   spring and fall. Write for detailed information.
2. The First United Presbyterian Church
   2910 Central Avenue, Middletown, OH 45042
   Weekend Healing Missions are conducted each
   spring. Write for registration information.
3. Dr. James K. Wagner
   First United Methodist Church
   2 South College Street, Athens, OH 45701
   Sponsors an annual healing mission. Write for
   information.
4. Dr. Ross Whetstone
   United Methodist Renewal Services Fellowship
   P. O. Box 50086, Nashville, TN 37205
   Schedules teaching conferences in various parts
   of the United States. Contact for dates and
   places.
5. International Order of St. Luke, the Physician
   61 Broad Street, Elizabeth, NJ 07201
   Schedules healing missions in various parts of
   the United States. Contact for dates and places.

APPENDIX E
Annotated Bibliography

Althouse, Lawrence W. *Rediscovering the Gift of Healing* Nashville: Abingdon, 1977.

A United Methodist minister discusses recent scientific research and experiments in healing, psychological and spiritual factors in physical illness, personal experiences in healing, and a working hypothesis and theology of healing.

Baillie, D. M. *God Was in Christ.* New York: Charles Scribner's Sons, 1948.

(an essay on incarnation and atonement)

With clarity and insight, the author discusses the classical interpretations of these two foundational Christian doctrines; basic reading for every serious student of Christology. Baille's "Tale of God" in the epilogue is worth the price of the book in itself.

Bartow, Don. *The Adventures of Healing.* Canton, Ohio: Life Enrichment Publishers, 1970.

A loose-leaf notebook with a wealth of material concerning the ministry of healing. A new article is written and mailed to readers on the mailing list each month.

_____."Beginning the Healing Ministry," "The Healing Service," "The Healing Mission," (three booklets) Canton, Ohio: Life Enrichment Publishers, 1964.

For a complete catalog, write: P. O. Box 526 Canton, OH 44701.

Basham, Don. *Deliver Us from Evil.* Old Tappan, New Jersey: Fleming H. Revell, 1972.

Those interested in modern exorcism will be enlightened by the deliverance ministry of this Christian Church minister.

Bennett, George. *The Heart of Healing.* Valley Forge: Judson Press, 1972.

This is a good introduction to the healing ministry of the church, by an English clergyman who believes that through

132

this ministry lay people are brought into an active, purposeful membership in the life and witness of the church.

Bonnell, John Sutherland. *Do You Want to Be Healed?* New York: Harper and Row, 1968.

Recommended reading for everyone in the healing ministry as well as curious Christians.

Browning, Don S. *Atonement and Psychotherapy.* Philadelphia: Westminster Press, 1966.

Browning tests the possibility of making positive theological statements on the basis of insights derived from psychotherapy, the focus of this study being Christ's death and resurrection. Reader needs to be familiar with psychotherapeutic terminology as well as atonement theories to grasp intent of the author.

Buttrick, George A. *Prayer.* New York: Abingdon-Cokesbury, 1942.

Prayer is a classic to be read by any student or practitioner of spiritual healing.

Cannon, Walter B. *Bodily Changes in Pain, Hunger, Fear, and Rage.* New York: D. Appleton and Company, 1929.

This Harvard University physiology professor demonstrates the relationship between certain elementary emotions and changes in bodily functions.

Carothers, Merlin R. *Prison to Praise: A Radical Prayer Concept for Changing Lives.* Plainfield, New Jersey: Logos International, 1970.

Written in an autobiographical style, this book reveals what happened in the life of the author (Methodist minister and Army chaplain) when he began to take seriously 1 Thessalonians 5:16-18, which reads:

"Rejoice evermore. Pray without ceasing. In everything give thanks: for this is the will of God in Christ Jesus concerning you!"

_____. *Answers to Praise: Letters to the Author of Prison to Praise.* Plainfield, New Jersey: Logos International, 1972.

A compilation from actual case histories of people who are learning the power of praising and thanksgiving.

_____. *Power in Praise: Sequel to Prison to Praise.* Plainfield, New Jersey: Logos International, 1972.

This book discusses how the spiritual dynamic of praise revolutionizes lives.

Cobb, E. Howard. *Christ Healing.* Irvington, New Jersey: St. Luke's Press, 1975.

Originally printed in 1933, this early work by an English

clergyman makes a timely contribution with its sane and balanced approach to "divine healing."

Colaw, Emerson S. *Thoughts on Divine Healing.* Nashville: Upper Room, 1972.

A concerned pastor (United Methodist) shares his insights and experience in the healing ministry of the church.

Colson, Charles W. *Born Again.* Old Tappan, New Jersey: Fleming H. Revell, 1976.

This is a truly remarkable story of a spiritual rebirth and personal healing by one of the men convicted in the Watergate scandal of the early 1970s.

Day, Albert E. *Letters on the Healing Ministry.* Nashville: Upper Room, 1964.

By using personal letters, the author addresses many subjects within the arena of spiritual healing with a convincing style.

Dunbar, Flanders. *Emotions and Bodily Changes.* New York: Columbia University Press, 1954.

As a survey of literature on psychosomatic interrelationships from 1910 to 1953, this is a classic in the scientific study of bodily changes that accompany emotions.

Duncombe, David C. *The Shape of the Christian Life.* Nashville: Abingdom, 1969.

Few books attempt to describe the mature Christian life. This author does a commendable job in presenting a positive portrait of a growing, effective Christian.

Dunnam, Maxie. *Dancing at My Funeral.* Nashville: Upper Room, 1973.

Excellent discussion is presented of ways to die to the old self in order to experience new life in Christ.

_____. *The Workbook of Living Prayer.* Nashville: Upper Room, 1975.

Exactly what the title implies, a personal workbook for a six-week, below-the-surface study of prayer and praying. Highly recommended to all who want to develop their inner life of the spirit.

_____. *Barefoot Days of the Soul.* Waco, Texas: Word Books, 1976.

This thesis concerns wholeness with commitment to Christ, the Liberator-Deliverer-Healer-Savior. By sharing his own faith-history, the author enables the reader to experience spiritual wholeness.

_____. *The Workbook of Intercessory Prayer.* Nashville: Upper Room, 1979.

This seven-week study on intercession not only examines

the hard questions related to prayer, but also offers an abundance of practical prayer exercises.

Grantham, Rudolph E. *The Healing Relationships.* Nashville: Upper Room, 1972.

Grantham helps the reader understand the conditions of illness as well as the conditions of reconciled, restored relationships.

Guidelines: The United Methodist Church and the Charismatic Movement.

Available from Discipleship Resources, P.O. Box 840, Nashville, TN 37202.

This position paper approved by the General Conference of the United Methodist Church in 1976 is "must" reading for every United Methodist concerned about the current interest in charismatic renewal efforts.

He Is Able, is ecumenical in nature, a quarterly journal dedicated to the restoration of the Ministry of Healing. Published by: He Is Able, Inc.

       220 Creath Street
       Box 1264
       Jonesboro, AR 72401

Hoyer, Robert. *Seventy Times Seven.* Nashville: Abingdon, 1976.

Because an unforgiving spirit blocks wholeness and health, the subject of forgiveness needs to be taken seriously by every Christian. The author offers simple exercises in the practice of forgiveness in everyday situations.

Keck, L. Robert. *The Spirit of Synergy (God's Power and You).* Nashville: Abingdon, 1978.

This book on meditative prayer deals not only in theory but also in specific techniques and is a welcome addition to the "meditation literature."

Kelsey, Morton T. *Healing and Christianity.* New York: Harper Row, 1973.

This foundational work shows historically, psychologically, and in relation to modern medical practices, the meaning that spiritual healing can have for contemporary Christians.

_____. *The Other Side of Silence: A Guide to Christian Meditation.* New York: Paulist Press, 1976.

The author, an Episcopal priest, makes a valuable contribution to the literature in this field. He not only surveys the various types of non-Christian meditation, but he also gives a sound rationale and several exercises for persons wanting to practice Christian meditation.

Kimmel, Jo. *Steps to Prayer Power.* Nashville: Abingdon, 1972.

Outstanding insights into the nature of prayer are revealed. The reader is provided with many "handles" to get hold of this universal, spiritual resource.

_____. *Stop Playing Pious Games.* Nashville: Abingdon, 1974.

The author challenges those who believe they have all the answers down pat, or who have fit everything neatly in a little box labeled "doctrine," or who have gotten into a spiritual rut, or who are eager to grow into maturity as sons and daughters of God and coheirs with Jesus Christ.

Kinghorn, Kenneth Cain. *Fresh Wind of the Spirit.* Nashville: Abingdon, 1975.

This is a readable book on the work of the Holy Spirit written for lay persons which takes into account both Holy Scripture and the best thinking of the church.

_____. *Gifts of the Spirit.* Nashville: Abingdon, 1976.

Kinghorn writes with a desire to help quell division among Christians, whether actual or potential. He provides a clear distinction between gifts and fruit of the spirit.

Knight, James A. *A Psychiatrist Looks at Religion and Health.* Nashville: Abingdon, 1964.

The author has the unique distinction of being both a psychiatrist and a clergyman. He surveys fifty years of discussions on this subject beginning with Freud, and is enthusiastic about the possibilities of religious-psychiatric teamwork, especially in the healing and care of the dying.

Kuhn, Barbara. *The Whole Lay Ministry Catalog.* New York: The Seabury Press (A Crossroad Book), 1979.

This unusual and unique catalog is designed to assist people in discovering their own spiritual gifts and role in the ministry of the church. The two chapters on prayer and healing are outstanding.

Langford, Thomas A. *Christian Wholeness.* Nashville: Upper Room, 1978.

Here is devotional writing at its best, graced by simplicity, but grounded in a profound and coherent theology. It can be used as a book of meditations or in a group study following the discussion guide.

Leslie, Robert C. *Health, Healing, and Holiness.* Nashville: Graded Press (United Methodist), 1971.

A study booklet written for adult groups in the church with teaching-learning suggestions for the leader at the end of each chapter. It is a good introduction to the subject of wholistic health and the unique resources within the Christian community.

Linn, Dennis, and Linn, Matthew. *Healing of Memories.* New York: Paulist Press, 1975.

The authors describe a journey and a process (inner healing) that can bring the reader into a deeper love of God, others, self.

MacNutt, Francis, O.P. *Healing.* Notre Dame, Indiana: Ave Maria Press, 1974.

Written by a Roman Catholic priest, this basic book is highly recommended as "a first reader" on the subject of spiritual healing. It discusses four different types of healing and how to pray for each. Excellent chapters are included on the relation of medicine to healing and why some people are not healed.

_____. *The Power to Heal.* Notre Dame, Indiana: Ave Maria, 1977.

In this sequel to *Healing,* Father MacNutt continues to share with the reader what he is learning in the healing ministry. Here is another outstanding book, written in honest, easy-to-understand language.

Manna, a periodical of the United Methodist Renewal Services Fellowship, is published at least six times annually for all persons interested in and committed to the renewal movement within the United Methodist Church. Write to:

UMRSF
Box 50086
Nashville, TN 37205

Marshall, Catherine. *Adventures in Prayer.* Old Tappan, New Jersey: Distributed by Fleming H. Revell Company, 1975.

Included here are very helpful discussions with examples of eight different kinds of prayer.

_____. *The Helper.* Waco, Texas: Chosen Books, 1978.

Recommended to anyone desiring insights into the Third Person of the Trinity.

McCausland, G. V. *Prayer-centered Listening.* Pittsburgh, Pennsylvania: R. T. Lewis Company, 1969.

The content consistently aims toward the spiritual-feeling level where the author believes people really live. Especially helpful to Christian counselors who counsel with Christians.

McMillin, S. I. *None of These Diseases.* Westwood, New Jersey, Fleming H. Revell Company, 1963.

Written by a Christian physician, this book traces biblical teachings in the prevention and treatment of disease.

Menninger, Karl. *Whatever Became of Sin?* New York: Hawthorne Books, Inc. 1973.

This reputable psychiatrist urges the clergy to affirm their unique calling and to preach comfort, repentance, hope, along with the forgiveness of sin.

Miller, Keith. *Please Love Me.* Waco, Texas: Word Books, 1977.

This is a true story of one woman's silent plea for the miracle of intimacy. This powerful narrative describes the inter-relatedness between emotional-spiritual-physical health and our need to love and to be loved.

Mills, Watson E. *Understanding Speaking in Tongues.* Grand Rapids, Michigan: Wm. B. Eerdmans Publishing Company, 1972.

Mills gives a balanced presentation on this highly controversial gift of the Spirit, calling for constructive dialogue between the glossolaliacs and the non-glossolaliacs. He pleads to exercise mutual tolerance, understanding, and Christian love.

Moffatt, Doris. *Christian Meditation (The Better Way).* Chappaqua, New York: Christian Herald Books, 1979.

This book is born out of the personal experience of a Christian woman who found that the practice of Christian meditation enables her to "put it all together" amidst the nitty-gritty of everyday life. It contains successful helps, prayer techniques, and specific meditations.

Morris, Danny E. *A Life That Really Matters.* Nashville: Discipleship Resources, 1973. Address: P. O. Box 840, Nashville, TN 37202.

This true story tells what happened in the life of the John Wesley United Methodist Church, (Tallahassee, Florida) when a small group began to follow intentionally five spiritual disciplines for one month. Sam E. Teague has written the companion piece, "The John Wesley Great Experiment," recommended as a short-term spiritual growth group discipline.

_____. *The Intensive Care Unit.* Discipleship Resources, P. O. Box 840, Nashville, TN, 37202.

Here is a five-week small group experience designed to help Christians be intentional in their caring ministries. A leader's guide is included.

Neal, Emily G. *A Reporter Finds God through Spiritual Healing.* New York: Morehouse-Barlow, 1965.

In the process of investigating spiritual healing, a skeptical reporter becomes a believer.

Nouwen, Henri. *The Wounded Healer.* Garden City, New York: Doubleday & Company, 1972.
_____. *Reaching Out: The Three Movements of the Spiritual Life.* Garden City, New York: Doubleday & Company, 1975.
_____. *The Living Reminder (Service and Prayer in Memory of Jesus Christ.)* New York: Seabury Press, 1977.
    The author's unique style and solid content make all of his books well worth the reading and contemplation.
Ogilvie, Lloyd John. *You've Got Charisma!* Nashville: Abingdon, 1975.
    This Presbyterian minister attempts quite successfully to recover the New Testament concept of charisma.
Parkhurst, Genevieve. *Healing The Whole Person.* New York: Morehouse-Barlow, 1968.
    The authority of Christ's healings for today is set forth by authentic witnesses to His powerful love. This book is an absorbing adventure for all those asking how it is possible.
Parkinson, George. *Spiritual Healing.* New York: Hawthorn Books, 1971.
    As pastor of a large Presbyterian church in Canton, Ohio, the author has been a pioneer in the healing ministry of the church. Here he shares a depth of understanding, a balance of judgement, and a ring of credibility needed in the growing literature on the subject.
Pipkin, H. Wayne. *Christian Meditation: Its Art and Practice.* New York: Hawthorn Books, 1977.
    Highly recommended for the beginner, this primer is useful for private as well as group meditations. The annotated bibliography is exceptional.
Price, Alfred W. "Religion and Health: A Guide for the Practice of Spiritual Healing"
    "Ambassadors of God's Healing" (a handbook for the practice of the Church's Ministry of Healing)
    These and several other excellent booklets are available
by contacting: St. Stephen's Episcopal Church
                  Tenth Street, Above Chestnut
                  Philadelphia, PA 19187
The Alfred W. Price Healing Collection is located in the B. L. Fisher Library, Asbury Theological Seminary, Wilmore, Kentucky.
Pruyser, Paul W. *Between Belief and Unbelief.* New York: Harper & Row, 1974.
    The author pleads for tolerance, respect, and understanding among persons of divergent belief systems, defining the

tensions to be dealt with. Recommended for the serious agnostic as well as the serious believer.

Roberts, Oral. *The Miracle of Seed Faith.* Tulsa, Oklahoma: Oral Roberts Publisher, 1970.

_____. *A Daily Guide to Miracles.* Tulsa, Oklahoma: Oral Roberts Publisher, 1975.

_____. *Better Health and Miracle Living.* Tulsa, Oklahoma: Oral Roberts Publisher, 1976.

Strong biblical teaching coupled with numerous true-life stories gives overwhelming witness to the abundant life possible in Jesus Christ.

Sanford, Agnes. *The Healing Light.* Macalester Park Publishing Company, 1947

Sanford writes one of the most influential books in the area of spiritual healing. Mrs. Sanford, for many years, has been a teacher of teachers in this field.

_____. *The Healing Gifts of the Spirit.* New York: Lippincott, 1966.

A practical and sensible guide to spiritual healing by one eminently qualified to write on the subject.

_____. *The Healing Power of the Bible.* New York: Lippincott, 1969.

An intermediate text for those who want to go beyond the basic ABC's of spiritual healing.

Sanford, John A. *Healing and Wholeness.* New York: Paulist Press, 1977.

The author's anecdotal style coupled with a working knowledge of his subject makes this enjoyable reading. It is one of the best presentations on the relationship between medicine, religion, and psychology.

Scanlan, Michael. *Inner Healing.* New York: Paulist Press, 1974.

A practical approach deals with the ministry and the minister of inner healing.

Selye, Hans. *Stress without Distress.* New York: Lippincott, 1974.

The goal is not to avoid stress (which is impossible); rather, to avoid stress becoming distress. Selye writes a significant book in helping us understand not only the relationship between stress and health, but also the importance of one's attitude toward stress, and how negative emotions increase distress while positive emotions are less stressful and more conducive to good health.

Sharing, a Journal of Christian Healing. Published ten times a year at 1161 East Jersey Street, Elizabeth, NJ 07201.

Sharing is an interdenominational, international magazine dedicated to Christian healing of the whole person (body, mind, and soul) and of situations. Published by the Order of St. Luke, the Physician.

Shlemon. Barbara L.; Linn, Dennis (S. J.) and Linn, Matthew (S. J.). *To Heal as Jesus Healed.* Notre Dame, Indiana: Ave Maria, 1978.

Catholics and non-Catholics alike will enjoy and reap many benefits from this in-depth discussion of the rite of the anointing Sacrament.

_____. *Healing Prayer.* Notre Dame, Indiana: Ave Maria, 1975.

This registered nurse writes with a childlike simplicity about effectiveness in prayers for healing. The chapters on forgiveness and inner healing are especially helpful.

Shostrom, Everett L. and Montgomery, Dan. *Healing Love: How God Works within the Personality.* Nashville: Abingdon, 1978.

Written by Christian psychologists, this book is a unique integration of depth psychology with practical Christian spirituality. The ultimate healing power of God's love is vividly illustrated in actual case histories and by the powerful personal witnesses of the two authors.

Stahl, Carolyn. *Opening to God.* Nashville: Upper Room, 1977.

An excellent book loaded with guided imagery meditations based on the Holy Scriptures.

Stanger, Frank B. *God's Healing Community.* Nashville: Abingdon, 1978.

This book contains a practical, detailed discussion of the biblical roots and the contemporary relevance of the church's healing ministry, most valuable to everyone who feels the church should be more active in the healing ministry. Ways to begin such a ministry in the local church are suggested. Questions for reflection lend themselves to a group study of this helpful work.

Stapleton, Ruth Carter. *The Gift of Inner Healing.* Waco, Texas: Word Books, 1976.

Tells how the author and others have been healed and helped to grow toward wholeness through relational experiences with Jesus Christ. This is a convincing discussion of how by "faith-imagination" one can experience inner healing or healing of memories.

_____. *The Experience of Inner Healing.* Waco, Texas: Word Books, 1977.

The reader is introduced to some methods of replacing

negative memories with God-inspired reconstruction of those memories. Stapleton provides ways of transforming past failures into positive stepping stones to Christlike wholeness.

Swaim, Loring T. *Arthritis, Medicine and the Spiritual Laws.* New York: Chilton Company, 1962.

An important contribution to psychosomatic medicine deserving careful study by practicing physicians and by pastoral counselors. The author, a medical doctor, is convinced that emotional stress can be a causative factor in rheumatoid arthritis and in other organic diseases.

Tournier, Paul. *The Healing of Persons.* New York: Harper & Row, 1965.

This renowned Swiss physician and psychiatrist treats the patient as a person, relating physical health to healing of the mind and the spirit. This book is a noteworthy contribution to a synthesis of modern psychology and the Christian religion.

Tuttle, Robert G., Jr. *The Partakers: Holy Spirit Power for Persevering Christians.* Nashville: Abingdon, 1974.

The Partakers is designed to help all Christians partake of the Holy Spirit and His gifts in the everydayness of life's struggles.

Weatherhead, Leslie D. *Psychology, Religion and Healing.* Nashville: Abingdon, 1951.

Here is a highly respected, critical study of all the non-physical methods of healing, with an examination of the principles underlying them and the techniques employed to express them, together with some conclusions regarding further investigation.

_____. *The Will of God.* Nashville: Abingdon, 1944.

This short book (only 56 pages) provides a useful and logical thesis on understanding God's will.

Westberg, Granger E. *Good Grief.* Philadelphia: Fortress Press, 1962.

The various stages in grief and adjustment are traced. A helpful book to place in the hands of grieving persons, and a constructive approach to the problem of loss.

_____. *Theological Roots of Wholistic Health Care,* 1979. Distributed by:

Wholistic Health Centers, Inc.
137 South Garfield
Hinsdale, IL 60521

Here is a report and reflection on what we are learning in and through the operation of wholistic health care centers

GRACE

(the painting on the front cover)

In this painting, I have sought to express my experience of God's love as stated in the hymn "I Sought the Lord." One day I was overwhelmed by the realization that while I sought the Lord, all along he was seeking me.

I sought the Lord, and afterward I knew
    He moved my soul to seek him, seeking me;
It was not I that found, O Savior true;
    No, I was found of thee.

Thou didst reach forth thy hand and mine enfold;
    I walked and sank not on the storm-vexed sea;
'Twas not so much that I on thee took hold
    As thou, dear Lord, on me.

I find, I walk, I love, but oh, the whole
    Of love is but my answer, Lord, to thee!
For thou wert long beforehand with my soul;
    Always thou lovedst me. Amen.

Though I was not thinking of healing when I did this painting, I am delighted that it is being used on the cover of this book. The ministry of healing is a manifestation of the grace and power of God's love in our lives.

The painting captures the moment of my response to God's love, which is always a healing experience.

Jerry Dunnam

situated in local churches. A quarterly newsletter is also available.

White, Anne S. *Healing Adventure: Understanding Divine Healing.* Plainfield, New Jersey: Logos, 1969.

White emphasizes the responsibility of the church today in providing healing ministries, and covers a wide range of subjects. Recommended as "a first book" to read for those new to spiritual healing.

Williams, Daniel D. *The Minister and the Care of Souls.* New York: Harper and Brothers, 1961.

Analysis of the pastoral tasks through the eyes of a theologian. The chapter on the sacraments is especially insightful for those involved in the healing ministry. To participate in the Holy Communion is to bring a corrective to the ever-present tendency to self-centeredness in our search for health. Forgiveness is seen as a releasing power offered through Christ's atonement.

Wise, Robert L. *When There Is No Miracle.* Glendale, California: Regal Books Division, G/L Publications, 1977.

Wise offers a clear and comforting word to help any believer walk through trouble and trauma at those times when pain and tragedy seemingly go unanswered and unexplained.

Wood, Robert. *A Thirty-Day Experiment in Prayer.* Nashville: Upper Room, 1978.

Here is practical help on beginning and keeping a personal prayer journal for one month. Because most healing is a long-term process, this is one way to make daily entries for later reflection and observation of God's love, care, and wholeness in our lives.